\ Amazing ! /
The secret of Hakkoryu Jujutsu

Explains its system of accelerated mastery

Controls the attacker using a single finger through mental effect

Supervisor: Hakkoryu 2nd Soke, Okuyama Ryuho
Editor: Monthly HIDEN editorial department
Translator: Kurabe Makoto Shiseido
Translation collaborator: Andrew Bryant

BAB JAPAN

**Amazing！The Secret of Hakkoryu Jujutsu
Explains its system of accelerated mastery**

Supervisor: Hakkoryu 2nd Soke, Okuyama Ryuho
Editor: Monthly HIDEN editorial department
Translator: Kurabe Makoto Shiseido
Translation collaborator: Andrew Bryant

Interior Design: Hitoshi Izumi

Copyright © 2017 BAB JAPAN

All rights reserved including the right of reproduction in whole or in part in any form.

ISBN978-4-8142-0060-3

Published by BAB JAPAN CO.,LTD
30-11 SASAZUKA 1-CHOME, SHIBUYAKU, TOKYO 151-0073 JAPAN
Tel.03-3469-0135 Fax.03-3469-0162
E-mail.shop@bab.co.jp
URL.http://www.bab.co.jp/
   http://budojapan.com/
   http://webhiden.jp/

Preface

By Hakkoryu 2nd Soke, Okuyama Ryuho

Between 2008 and 2014, a series of articles were published in the Japanese martial arts journal Hiden, which introduced our Hakkoryu Jujutsu to its readers. Because the editors of Hiden had received a lot of impressive reaction from the readers they decided to publish these articles as a book. In this way they published this book, which consists of the essence of that series of articles that described Hakkoryu Jujutsu.

Our Hakkoryu has the formal name of Nippon Bugei Tsukasa Goshindo Hakkoryu Jujutsu (日本武芸司護身道八光流柔術) which translates as "Japanese traditional self-defense martial art of the Eighth-Lights System".

In the past, before the Second World War (WWII), our dojo (named 八光流講武塾Hokkoryu Koubu Juku) was located at the Kanda Otamagaike (神田お玉が池), area of Tokyo. This place is quite famous among bujutsu enthusiasts because the Genbukan Dojo (玄武館道場) of the famous Hokushin Itto-ryu school of Kenjutsu (北辰一刀流剣術) was located there at the end of the Tokugawa Shogunate (1603 to 1868). That dojo was crowded, with a lot of visitors who wished to receive our founder's instruction. Almost every day the dojo was filled with around 150 people who came, not only from Japan, but from other Asian countries. The training was done one-on-one, through private instruction with the founder. Because it was on a "first come, first served" basis, every day visitors waited in a long line in front of the dojo building.

The founder, 1st Soke Okuyama Ryuho, taught his students using this one-on-one teaching method, which utilizes every minute for the direct transfer of knowledge from teacher to student. He never wasted time in vain, like instructing, then waiting, or pausing as students practiced, which was done in most of other schools at that time. During class time, he tried all his best to teach his students "how to save oneself from potential danger". This could be the reason why he attracted so many people wishing to learn our Hakkoryu.

It is a remarkable feature of Hakkoryu that people can practice the entire curriculum, even in such a small area as $2m^2$. Accordingly, everyone can practice Hakkoryu anytime, anywhere, as our founder instructed. And in this way people can regard Hakkoryu as a Bujutsu on which people can dedicate their highest effort to master.

I often receive reports from my students who had occasion to defend himself/herself against violence thanks to Hakkoryu's techniques, through which one can control the attacker, even using a single finger. Because our Hakkoryu does not specialize in brutal techniques such as striking and kicking, but rather, offers a more sophisticated system, a lot of people are attracted to it as a modern method of self-defense to be used as a means of physical and mental training.

When a person masters Hakkoryu he/she should notice the effect that an aggressive heart will become more peaceful, a timid heart will become braver, and thick-headed person can become a wiser person. Also, an indecisive person can learn to make a more decisive decision, and a lethargic person can become quite energetic, thanks to the result of training diligently in Hakkoryu.

In Hakkoryu, we reject all types of fighting methods that use any type of weapon, and we teach people how to defend themselves against violence by cultivating minds and moral character, through the course of mastering this system. In fact, once one starts learning Hakkoryu, he/she should begin improving his/her physical appearance from the effect of changing on the inside (the mind).

Here, I write the message that our founder sent to all the people who attempt to master Hakkoryu.

"If our Hakkoryu can help those people who try to establish a resolute and stable personality, filled with hopes and ideals, I feel happiest. If you are a person who cannot pretend to not see the actual world, with a lot of wickedness, come and join us. Hakkoryu shall guide you to a place where you feel "you do not need to search, but you earn what is valuable to you for yourself."

Table of contents

		page
Preface		3
Introduction	**History of Hakkoryu, i.e. the biography of the founder Okuyama Ryuho, 1st Soke**	6
Summary	**Its sophisticated technical hierarchy and teaching system**	10
Chap 1	**To raise your hand as if to scratch your itchy ear**	30
Chap 2	**Imagine yourself as a great Buddha statue**	38
Chap 3	**Do not resist, then you can realize the techniques**	46
Chap 4	**Do nothing except drop yourself with gravity**	54
Chap 5	**Open my hand in the Hakko shape**	62
Chap 6	**The secret of "pain"**	70
Chap 7	**About Kamae (Posturing)**	78
Chap 8	**The importance of "fingers" and their strongest direction**	86
Chap 9	**Danger arises suddenly without time to prepare**	94
Chap 10	**One can only concentrate for a short time**	102
Chap 11	**The technique of guiding your opponent to do what you intend**	114
Chap 12	**Goshin Taiso (selfdefense physical exercise)**	122
Chap 13	**The teaching contained in escaping from a bound rope**	132
Chap 14	**Resuscitation Methods**	140
Chap 15	**Never do it too much**	150
Chap 16	**"Front"**	160
Chap 17	**Where am I?**	168
Chap 18	**San Dai Kichu (Three Great Pillars)**	176
Supplement	**How to defend yourself using a one finger strike**	184
Conclusion		198

Introduction

History of Hakkoryu, i.e. the biography of the founder Okuyama Ryuho, 1st Soke.

◈ About the founder Okuayama Ryuho 1st Soke

The founder of Hakkoryu Jujutsu was born in Yamagata prefecture in December 1901. From his birth, he suffered from a physically weak condition and he fell seriously ill with meningitis when he was 5 years old. At that time his life was saved by an herbalist named Mr. Tahara. This experience became the trigger that attracted him to oriental medicine in the future. After recovering from meningitis, he still suffered from several serious illnesses, one after another during his childhood, and because of these difficult experiences he vowed to help cure others who were suffering from the same difficulties as he had.

Because of his weakness, due to illnesses, he was behind his colleagues for several years in his school studies. In 1922 he left home and moved to Asahikawa in Hokkaido so that he could begin studying political science and public speaking. In 1925 he moved to Tokyo and entered a school located in Tokyo where they taught politics

In 1927 he graduated from that school and went back to Asahikawa, where he organized the Northern Japan public speaking Union. He became active making public speeches to enlighten people about politics and he also established the Youth Congress of public speaking, together with 80 other young men with the same intention.

At that time he also started Bujutsu practice (martial arts) together with his political activities. He practiced Daito-ryu Jujutsu with Matsuda Toshimi-sensei and later, under master Takeda Sokaku-sensei. Then later he travelled all over Japan, from north to south, to such places as Teshio, Nigata, Kyoto,

Introduction
History of Hakko-ryu, i.e. the biography of the founder Okuyama Ryuho, 1st Soke.

The founder Okuyama Ryuho, 1st Soke

At Left: Okuyama Ryuho, 1st Soke, when he was a student at the Politics School of Tokyo.

At Right: Okuyama Ryuho, 1st Soke, when he was operating his Koho Shiatsu school. To his left side is Mr. Ichiki, who contributed to the spread of Koho Shiatsu on Karafuto Island.

Miyatsu, Ise, Kumamoto and Okinawa, to meet masters of various kinds of Bujutsu, aside from his Daito-ryu studies. But eventually he found that none of these styles he had studied was the exact one he wished to master.

He studied medicine with Dr. Hirata Ryozan of Dai Tomeisha, and also studied both Psychology and oriental medicine with Dr. Minami Haizan, president of Oriental Medicine Association. He mastered several kinds of medicine, which would later become the basis of his future Koho Shiatsu method, but he felt something did not quite fit with what he learned at that time. The clearest difference is the way the affected area is approached. For instance, Dr. Hirata stimulated the affected area directly, but conversely, the founder established a way to heal the affected area by not touching it directly. This became the very basic concept of Koho Shiatsu. He studied the relationship among the organs of the human body quite deeply, and as a result he developed the concept of approaching the affected area indirectly.

Later he recollected, in his respect to his teachers, as follows.

"What I established seems like a rebellion against my teachers. But because of the fact that I could learn my teachers' great concepts, I was able to go on to further develop these concepts and eventually make their teachings more complete. As a result of my research, so many sick people have been cared for by my Koho Shiatsu method and, although my teachers have already passed away, I hope they would find praise for me in this achievement."

The founder established the Koho school in Asahikawa to develop many physicians who could help cure the sick and ill using his Koho Shiatsu method. This activity has spread all over Japan, even as far as Karafuto, which is located further north of Hokkaido.

◈ Foundation of Hakkoryu

The founder, who had been studying both the martial arts and medicine together, was slowly starting to notice that both have a complementary relationship. He asked himself what is needed in society. This can just be "society" "Medicine is not enough. Besides medicine, the study of Bujutsu is necessary." This was his eventual conclusion.

During the period he lived in Hokkaido, he developed a friendship with Mr. Namikoshi Tokujiro, who would become a very famous teacher of Shiatsu later on. Both promised each other that Mr. Namikoshi would make his living as a healer, while the founder as a Bujutsu-ka, or a martial artist.

In 1941, the founder moved to Tokyo once again and, after establishing a temporary Dojo in Hongo, built a permanent three-story Dojo at Otamagaike, in Kanda. At that time we can say that Hakkoryu Jujutsu was founded.

The building consisted of the actual dojo on the basement floor, bedrooms and a tea ceremony room on the 1st floor, and the shiatsu training room on the 2nd floor. The founder maintained his strict teaching method of private one-on-one training, and this never changed, even when he gained a great number of students later on. Even today, Hakkoryu maintains the same teaching methodology.

In 1945 there was a great air raid in Tokyo that killed 150,000 people in a single night, and the founder's Dojo burned down. He then evacuated to Haguroyama in Yamagata prefecture where he was born, and in 1947 (after the war) he moved to Omiya City in Saitama prefecture, near Tokyo. It was here that he built a new Dojo. Since that time this Dojo has been the Headquarters of Hakkoryu.

Introduction
History of Hakko-ryu, i.e. the biography of the founder Okuyama Ryuho, 1st Soke.

After the founding of Hakkoryu, he continued to strictly adhere to the one-on-one teaching methodology. This teaching style has been maintained to this day.

Photo taken in June, 1942, at the occasion of the founding ceremony for Hakkoryu Jujutsu. In the first row wearing traditional formal clothes is the founder, and to his left side is Dr. Minami Haizan-sensei

Considering the path the founder followed, including his serious commitment to Politics and public speaking, his intense research of medicine, and mastering a Bujutsu with a strong philosophy of self-defense, everybody should realize that the one clear fundamental desire of the founder was to "Wish everyone to have stronger will/intention to live and accordingly can find better path."

This must be the true essence of Hakkoryu Jujutsu as a martial art.

The founder once described Hakkoryu as follows.

"By practicing Hakkoryu a person finds its concepts are similar to other traditional Japanese concepts. Then the person shall notice its concepts extend much wider to that of the actual living world (outside the Dojo). In Hakkoryu, neither the fantasy, nor imaginary world exists and no illogical or mysterious things exist. Everybody can just see everyday reality and normal life where the True Way of life exists."

In 1987 the founder passed away at the age of 85 years old. After that time, his son took over as Soke (headmaster) and has been continuing Hakkoryu as 2nd Soke, Okuyama Ryuho to the present day.

Summary

Its sophisticated technical hierarchy and teaching system

❁ "Spiral"

It has been mentioned that Hakkoryu Jujutsu resenbles Daito-ryu Aikijujutsu. This is not true, and Daito-ryu Aikijujutsu has no affiation with Hakkoryu.

On the other hand, in Hakkoryu, they do not use the word AIKI. And it is their premise that everybody can master all the listed techniques, in Hakkoryu.

The biggest difference between Hakkoryu and Daito-ryu exists in their curriculum. Please refer to [table 0-1], which shows the hierarchy of Hakkoryu techniques. Although not all techniques are listed here, the curriculum presented is still quite large.

The biggest surprise is that those techniques listed do not simply include variations, based on different attacks, or even alternate situations in which each technique could be applied.

The important meaning of this list is in the progression of its hierarchy. Actually, all these techniques are arranged in a spiral relationship. Generally speaking, in a spiral progression model, when one makes a complete revolution (circle) upwards, he/she does not come back to the exact same position where he/she started, but actually moves one level higher. That is spiral progression. In other words, when one practices each technique, he/she progress higher technically, step-by-step.

When people practice Shodan-Gi (1st Dan techniques) as beginners, in most cases, they do not have a clear idea of what they are doing. But when they reach Nidan-Gi (2nd Dan techniques), they start understanding each of the 1st Dan techniques much deeper than they did before. Then they gain a clearer understanding about what they are doing in previous techniques. In

Summary
Its sophisticated technical hierarchy and teaching system

such a way, they progress to 2nd Dan, then to 3rd Dan, and so forth. Finally they shall realize the fact that the techniques they initially learned at 1st Dan have the deepest meaning among all techniques.

Now people should better understand the spiral system of instruction (i.e. the syllabus arranged in an upward spiral progression), by which they do not progress in a straight line to the goal, but gradually move higher towards their goal, step-by-step, revolution-by-revolution.

Now, let's follow the progress of this spiral structured syllabus. First, let's trace a horizontal line in the list, from right (start) to left (end), which is the Japanese way of ordering and opposite from the European way (i.e., left to right).

Every beginner should learn the technique called Hakko Dori (Eighth-Light Art) as their first lesson. The basic sequence of its motion is that one raises both wrists and arms which are grasped by the opponent (refer to [illustration & photos 0-1]).

At just a glance, it looks like the hands are being raised to free the wrists, but releasing the wrists is just a result, not the goal. This technique is taught so that everyone can learn how to raise their hands/arms.

In the first place, it is not easy to raise the arm that is grasped at the wrist. Because I am involved in the editing of a martial arts journal, I often watch similar demonstrations, so I first thought this would not be very difficult. But when I tried it myself, I could not raise my hands/arms at all.

Then Okuyama 2nd Soke instructed me as follows:

"At first it is most important to keep your posture straight, as if your entire body is supported by a rigid steel bar. And you should relax your arms completely. Otherwise, unless you do so, and try to raise your arms using power, you can never raise them. You should create rising power from that part of the abdomen which is located between the belly and hips. You should put your consciousness into your abdomen and try to move your arms up towards your ears, but not try to consciously raise your hands/arms in the process."

After receiving this advice from Okuyama 2nd Soke, I tried again, and to my surprise, I could do it easily.

I realized that you practice this Hakko Dori technique to learn correct

Table of Hakkoryu Technical System

The techniques listed here from 1st Dan to 3rd Dan are general techniques. The techniques of 4th Dan are associate Shihan techniques, and for the Shihan level techniques, although only a part of them are listed, include all the techniques listed from 1st Dan to 4th Dan. Shihan techniques are classified into three sections. The 1st consists of all the techniques listed between 1st Dan and 4th Dan. The 2nd part consists of the 5th Dan techniques, such as specific the Dan level versions of Tekagami, Tsuki Mi Dori, Nukiuchi Dori etc. In addition, it includes the techniques of the 1st section, which add the "one point" or "one hand" secret method taught only by Souke as Kuden (oral tradition). The 3rd section of techniques are called Okuden (inner teachings), which includes the techniques that are not categorized in the 1st or 2nd sections, and

table 0-1

Shodan (1st Dan)

- **Suwari Waza (Seated Techniques)**
  Hakko Dori (Eighth-Light Art)
  Tekagami (Hand Mirror)
  Aiki Nage (Harmonious Spirit Throw)
  Hiza Gatame (Knee Hold)
  Ude Osae Dori (Arm Pin Art)
  Mune Osae Dori (Chest Pin Art)
  Uchikomi Dori (Strike Inside Art)
- **Hantachi Waza (Half-Standing Techniques)**
  Yoko Katate Osae Dori (Side One-Hand Art)
  Kiza Morote Osae Dori (Siting on Chair Two-Hands Pin Art)
  Tachi Waza (Standing Techniques)
  Hakko Zeme (Eighth-Light Attack)
  Tachi Ate (Standing Strike)
  Tachi Tekagami (Standing Hand Mirror)
  Hiki Nage (Pulling Throw)
  Ude Osae Dori (Arm Pin Art)
  Mune Osae Dori (Chest Pin Art)
  Ryou Ude Osae Dori (Double Arm Pin Art)
  Ryou Mune Osae Dori (Double Chest Pin Art)
  Uchikomi Dori (Strike Inside Art)
  Ushiro Zeme Otoshi (Rear Attack Drop)
  Kasa Ushiro Zeme Dori (Umbrella Rear Attack Art)
  Kubishime Dori (Strangulation Art)

Nidan (2nd Dan)

- **Suwari Waza (Seated Techniques)**
  Matsuba Dori (Pin Needle Art)
  Tekagami (Hand Mirror)
  Ude Osae Dori (Arm Pin Art)
  Mune Osae Dori (Chest Pin Art)
  Konoha Gaeshi (Leaf Turnover)
  Aya Dori (Woven Art)
  Uchikomi Dori (Strike Inside Art)
- **Hantachi Waza (Half-Standing Techniques)**
  Hantachi Mae Ryoute Osae Dori (Half-Standing Front Two-Hand Pin Art)
- **Tachi Waza (Standing Techniques)**
  Makikomi (Wrapping Inside)
  Shuto Jime (Sword-Hand Lock)
  Ryou Shuto Jime (Double Sword-Hand Lock)
  Tachi Tekagami (Standing Hand Mirror)
  Ude Osae Dori (Arm Pin Art)
  Mune Osae Dori (Chest Pin Art)
  Ryou Ude Osae Dori (Double Arm Pin Art)
  Ryou Mune Osae Dori (Double Chest Pin Art)
  Konoha Gaeshi (Leaf Turnover)
  Mune Konoha Gaeshi (Chest Leaf Turnover)
  Katate Osae Aya Dori (One-Hand Pin Woven Art)
  Uchikomi Dori (Strike Inside Art)
  Mae Nihou Nage (Front Two-Way Throw)
  Ushiro Nihou Nage (Rear Two-Way Throw)

Sandan (3rd Dan)

- **Suwari Waza (Seated Techniques)**
  Ude Osae Dori (Arm Pin Art)
  Mune Osae Dori (Chest Pin Art)
  Uchikomi Dori (Strike Inside Art)
  Tekagami (Hand Mirror)
  Aya Dori (Woven Art)
- **Hantachi Waza (Half-Standing Techniques)**
  Yoko Dori (Side Art)
  Morote Osae Dori (Two-Hand Pin Art)
  Ushiro Gyaku Kubishime Dori (Rear Reverse Strangulation Art)
- **Tachi Waza (Standing Techniques)**
  Ryou Mune Osae Dori (Double Chest Pin Art)
  Emon Dori (Clothing Art)
  Tachi Tekagami (Standing Hand Mirror)
  Uchikomi Dori (Strike Inside Art)
  Tsukimi Dori (Body Thrust Art)
  Kata Mune Osae Mochi Mawari (One Side Chest Pin Lead Around)
  Ryoute Mochi Mawari (Two-Hand Lead Around)
  Ushiro Zeme Dori (Rear Attack Art)
  Ushiro Emon Dori (Rear Clothing Art)
  Ushiro Obi Hiki Dori (Rear Belt Pull Art)
  Mae Obi Hiki Dori (Front Belt Pull Art)
  Nukiuchi Dori (Quick Strike Art)
  Tsukikomi Dori (Thrust Inside Art)
  Ushiro Hakko Dori (Rear Eighth-Light Art)

Yondan (4th Dan)

- **Suwari Waza (Seated Techniques)**
  Mune Dori (Chest Art)
  Ude Dori (Arm Art)
  Emon Dori (Clothing Art)
  Tekagami (Hand Mirror)
- **Hantachi Waza (Half-Standing Techniques)**
  Yoko Dori (Side Art)
  Yoko Ninin Dori (Side Two-Person Art)
- **Tachi Waza (Standing Techniques)**
  Mune Dori (Chest Art)
  Ushiro Zeme Dori (Rear Attack Art)
  Ushiro Hakko Dori (Rear Eighth-Light Art)

Summary
Its sophisticated technical hierarchy and teaching system

also very sophisticated techniques. Then for Kaiden (highest level) techniques, the techniques listed here are the same as all the techniques listed from 1st Dan to 5th Dan, but with certain special mental effects added. The differences are difficult to notice only by watching. Like the previous Shihan level, Kaiden techniques also include Okuden techniques that are not categorized in the previous techniques from 1st Dan to 5th Dan, and consist of highly advanced and complex techniques. The three great foundation pillars are the ultimate secret of Hakkoryu. In fact, if one wishes to perform all the techniques perfectly, he/she should master these three great foundation pillars.

Uchikomi Dori (Strike Inside Art)
Yokomen Uchi Dori (Side of Head Strike Art)
Oikake Dori (Pursuit Art)
Heiko Dori (Parallel Art)
Kote Gaeshi Dori (Wrist Reversal Art)
Shiraha Dori (White Sword Edge Art)
Daito Nukiuchi Dori (Long Sword Quick Strike Art)
Shoto Tsukikomi Dori (Short Sword Thrust Inside Art)

Shihan Waza (Model, or Master Instructor Techniques)
- **Shodan (1st dan)**
Hakko Dori (Eighth-Light Art)
Tekagami (Hand Mirror)
Yoko Dori (Side Art)
Ude Osae Dori (Arm Pin Art)
Mune Osae Dori (Chest Pin Art)
- **Nidan (2nd Dan)**
Shiho Nage (Four-Way Throw)
Ude Osae Dori (Arm Pin Art)
Mune Osae Dori (Chest Pin Art)
Maki Komi (Wrapping Inside)
Konoha Gaeshi (Leaf Turnover)
- **Sandan (3rd Dan)**
Emon Dori (Clothing Art)
Gakun (the action of the Gakun grip)
- **Yondan (4th Dan) (The Same; Ditto)**
- **Godan (5th Dan)**
Additional one hand and one point secret oral teachings
- **Okuden (Inner Teachings)**
Hagai Jime Dori (Rear Pinioning, or "Full-Nelson" Art)
Kubishime (Neck Strangulation)
Mune Dori Nage (Chest Seize Throw)

Kasa Osae Dori (Umbrella Pin Art)
Sensu Dori (Folding Fan Art)
Tsue Osae Dori (Walking Stick Art)
Katate Nage (One-Hand Throw)
Ninin Dori (Two-Person Art)
Yonin Dori (Four-Person Art)
Nawa Nuke (Rope Escape)

Kaiden Higi Sandaikichu (Highest Level Secret Teachings, Three Great Foundation Pillars)
- **Shodan (1st Dan)**
Hakko Dori (Eighth-Light Art)
Tekagami (Hand Mirror)
Ude Osae Dori (Arm Pin Art)
Mune Osae Dori (Chest Pin Art)
Yoko Dori (Side Art)
Nidan (2nd Dan)
Ude Osae Dori (Arm Pin Art)
Mune Osae Dori (Chest Pin Art)
Shiho Nage (Four-Way Throw)
Morote Shiho Nage (Two-Hand Four-Way Throw)
- **Sandan (3rd Dan)**
Emon Dori (Clothing Art)
- **Gakun (the action of the Gakun grip)**
- **Yondan, Godan (4th Dan, 5th Dan) (The Same; Ditto)**
- **Okuden (Inner Teachings)**
Mae Gyaku San Nage (Front Reverse Three Throw)
Ushiro Gyaku San Nage (Rear Reverse Three Throw)
Suwari Gyaku Go Nage (Seated Reverse Five Throw)
Tachi Gyaku Go Katame (Standing Reverse Five Hold)
Ishi Datami (Stone Mat)
Kougan Shibori (Testicle Squeeze)
Katana Tsuka Osae Dori (Sword Handle Pin Art)
Hosho Dori (Paper Art)
Hakko Nage (Eighth-Light Throw)
Katate Nage (One-Hand Throw)
Sai Rui (Tearing Up)
Fugi (Release Technique)
- **Kichu (Foundation Pillars)**
Roken Senretsu (Shoulder of the Road)
Kengai Kenshin (Seeing Truth at the Edge of the Cliff)
Shinki Yakujo (God Skin Illumination)

These great many techniques are arranged in a spiral fashion. One makes a single revolution but does not come back to the original point, rather, one step higher (like an upward reaching spiral). Thus, as one progresses forward along the horizontal line, they also progress upward along the vertical line automatically.

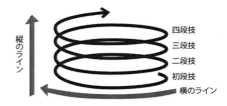

Horizontal line: illustration & photos 0-1

All beginners should start learning techniques in the order of: Hakko Dori, Tekagami (Hand Mirror), Aiki Nage (Harmonizing Throw)......which follows the horizontal line shown in [table 0-1]. Once one masters Hakko Dori, he is ready to master Tekagami. Once he masters Tekagami, then he is ready to master Aiki Nage. The technical structure is made up in such a way.

❶ Hakko-Dori

This can be regarded as the basis of all the techniques. At a glance it looks like a way to free your grasped wrists, but having your wrists grasped from above, it is not easy to raise them. The most important point is that one can raise their hands/arms from such a difficult situation. Namely photos 01-03 show the important part. One must relax their arms without putting power into them, and try to create power from the abdomen, which allows one to leverage power from all over their body. As a result, one can raise their hands/arms without much difficulty. This should be the basic method of all the techniques, in that one can raise their hands/arms which normally cannot be raised.

In Hakkoryu, it is instructed that one should move the hands up towards the ears as if he/she is going to scratch his/her ears (as if to scratch an itch). Normally, when one's wrist is grasped, he/she immediately applies power at that point, which causes the situation where he/she can never raise his/her hands or arms.

One must relax their arms without putting power into them, and try to create power from the abdomen. However, if one is too conscious of the abdomen, one tends to put power into their abdominal muscles, which is incorrect. One must relax the abdominal muscles, then put their consciousness on the point between the belly and waist (tanden).

Summary
Its sophisticated technical hierarchy and teaching system

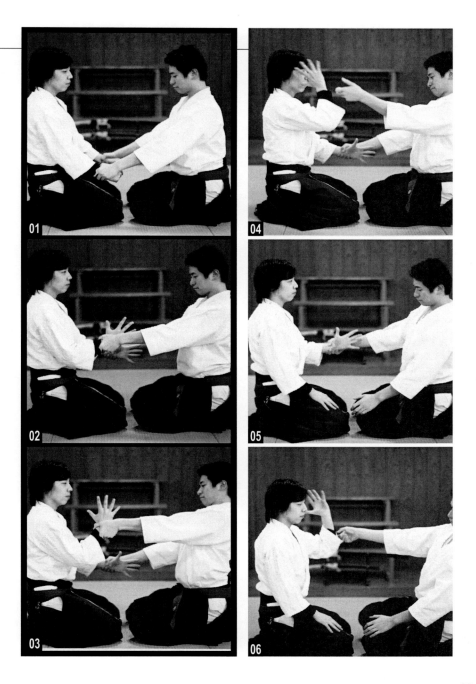

❷ Tekagami (Hand Mirror)

photos 0-2

Raise your hand with the palm facing your body, as a woman would using a compact mirror (as previously noted, Tekagami means "hand mirror") when they touch up their makeup. After mastering the raising hand and arm motion of Hakko Dori (photo no. 01-03), you can perform this motion, which is shown in photos no. 01-03. In this way, the order of the techniques is arranged. For this version of Tekagami, the important point is to drop the grasped hand, which is shown in [photos 0-3], no. 05 and 06. It looks as if he drops both hands together, but actually he drops only the right hand, with the left hand being attached to right hand, and through this motion, he can unbalance the opponent. It is very difficult to unbalance the opponent using only arm power. You should leverage the force of gravity.

posturing and to allow the hands and arms to be relaxed, without putting unnecessary power into them. Without mastering these basic points you can never progress further.

I was also surprised that I could do this so easily, although not on the first try. I was quite impressed with the excellent teaching skill of Okuyama 2nd Soke, and I well understood the fact that his standard teaching time per person is as short as 20 minutes. If he teaches in such a way, this is reasonably long enough and not too short.

After mastering this Hakko Dori, you progress to Tekagami (which means "compact mirror for women", please refer to [photos 0-2]).

The first three photos (no. 01-03) show the sequence of how to raise the hands/arms with the palms facing your body.

16

Summary
Its sophisticated technical hierarchy and teaching system

This motion can be done only after you have mastered Hakko Dori.

After raising your hands and arms, you shall unbalance the opponent. Normally, at this stage, one intends to "cut" the opponent's hand using his released hand ("cutting" with the edge of your hand in the shape of a blade), but the most important act is just before this "cutting" motion, which is shown in photos no.05 and 06.

At this stage, one unbalances the opponent as a preparation for the next step of "cutting". This unbalancing is not as easily done as it looks. If you try to pull down your grasped hand/arm with power, you cannot do it under strong resistance from the opponent. You can perform this motion only if you try to drop your grasped hand using gravity. Your arm's mass creates quite a strong dropping force with gravity, and you can only leverage or harness this if you avoid putting even a tiny bit of power in your arms.

After mastering this version of Tekagami you progress to the next technique of Aiki Nage. As mentioned before, we generally do not use the word "Aiki" in Hakkoryu. This case is the only exception, and the meaning of Aiki in Hakkoryu is not the same as used in Daito-ryu.

Aiki Nage starts with the motion of pulling down the grasped right wrist to the same side, as shown in photos no. 01 and 02. Of course, this motion can only be performed once you have mastered the

photos 0-3

❸ Aiki Nage

Unbalance the opponent by dropping the grasped hand in the manner one mastered in the previous technique of Tekagami. Only by performing that motion in Tekagami which is shown in photos no. 05 and 06, can you understand the dropping motion of Aiki Nage shown in photos no. 01 and 02. In this step, another motion is added to turn the opponent by leading him with your left hand/arm, as shown in photos no. 03 and 04. In Hakkoryu only this technique is the exception that contains the word "Aiki" in its name, but it does not have the same meaning as the one used in Daito-ryu.

For the motion shown in photos no. 02-04, you have to rotate your left hand while keeping the base of the thumb as the point of rotation. It will never work if you try to use arm or hand power to push the opponent in an effort to turn his body.

You should consciously move the little finger of your left hand, which you can still move a little bit, even in the situation of a strong grip, and then try to enlarge that motion to rotate your entire left hand.

dropping motion of Tekagami, which is shown in photos no. 05 and 06.

All the techniques are arranged in such a way that by mastering one, this leads to the mastering of the next. It does not matter if you are good or bad at one technique. If you master one step, you are surely well prepared to master the next step. The curriculum of Hakkoryu is this well thought out.

18

Summary
Its sophisticated technical hierarchy and teaching system

From another angle

05

06

07

08

◉ Progressing to a higher level:

Now let's observe the vertical line in the list of techniques shown on page 11. When you master all 1st Dan techniques and move up to the 2nd Dan techniques, you will encounter the same techniques that you mastered in the 1st Dan level. For instance, Tekagami, which you learned at the 1st Dan level, will be learned again in the 2nd, 3rd and 4th Dan levels, as well. But there is a clear difference among each Tekagami technique of the various different levels. The Tekagami of each Dan level has a different theme that is actually related to each other in a quite sophisticated way, as one completion creates the preparation for the next. While you make progress along the horizontal line of the technical structure, you also make progress along the vertical line without noticing it yourself. Only when you reach the next higher step and see what you have mastered in the previous level, will you notice that your basic level of skill overall is also now one step higher. At this point, you start to realize the hierarchy of Hakkoryu's systematic technical structure much clearer. After repeating those steps, you will eventually reach the highest level at the end of your "journey".

I received a special invitation from Okuyama 2nd Soke to watch the Okuden techniques. The techniques he demonstrated are fantastic. They, Hakko Dori, or

19

Gakun, and so on, look like a miracle, because I could never expect that such movements and their results could be possible, but he did them all so effortlessly. There are so many miraculous techniques in Hakkoryu, and the sophisticated combination of these makes Hakkoryu truly wonderful.

I heard Hakkoryu has self development principle which means a student must take initiative to learn something from a teacher. Students should approach an instructor themselves to ask for instruction, and then the teaching shall begin. Also, instructors take it upon themselves to let the student notice each important point clearly enough on their own, but then never leave these points unclear for the student.

I remember now that Koho Shiatsu also has the same concept. In Hakkoryu, each member is respected as an individual. They never force students to accept what the instructors teach them, but attempt to let them notice what is important for themselves.

Before my interview, I had imagined Hakkoryu Jujutsu with techniques causing extreme pain, its hidden secrets cloaked in a thick veil, and that they have a high handed way of teaching. But after finishing my interview and having a personal experience with the art, I realized that my preconceptions were completely wrong. Hakkoryu's three main ideas are: no challenge, no resistance and no injury. Accordingly it could not be high handed

Okuyama 2nd Soke says "Of course our techniques apply enormous pain, but if you can make yourself relaxed enough, you will never feel pain anymore."

By hearing this explanation I understood that in Hakkoryu, one can learn how to relax himself via learning how to reduce the pain he receives in a very practical way. I think this is quite profound.

Okuyama 2nd Soke said with a smile, "Although our techniques are quite energetic, the relationship between members is friendly. It is no use to make that relationship strict. We cherish smiling because it raises mental strength."

I found his smile quite attractive.

Its sophisticated technical hierarchy and teaching system

Vertical line:

The same technique changes its content as the technical level advances, such as 1st Dan, 2nd Dan, 3rd Dan... That is the "Vertical line". At 1st Dan the purpose is to master basic body mechanics and learn how to relax the muscles. Then, as the training level advances, a new theme is introduced, step-by-step, such as a new technical sequence being added, or the direction of applied power changes.

photos 0-4

Tekagami
(1st Dan level)

It is rather difficult to move the grasped hands together in the center and requires certain knowledge. You should relax enough and move both hands in a natural motion, without putting unnecessary power into the arms.

Never try to apply technique, but allow it work naturally. It is also important to keep proper posture. You should leverage power which is created—not from the arm—but from the whole body. You cannot perform this if you put even a small amount of power into your arm.

Tekagami
(2nd Dan level)

For Tekagami of 2nd Dan, an additional kime is added after executing the "cutting" motion.

Summary

Its sophisticated technical hierarchy and teaching system

Tekagami
(3rd Dan level)

For Tekagami of 3rd Dan, the unbalancing direction is changed from the outside to the inside. You cannot drop your arm down to unbalance the opponent just by using a simple physical twisting motion. There is an important theme here on how you can transfer your arm's weight to your opponent in order to unbalance and control him. After mastering this 3rd Dan version of Tekagami, you can now understand previous Tekagami techniques in a much deeper way than before.

Tekagami
(4th Dan level)

Here, the technique of Tekagami varies quite a lot. The raising motion of the grasped wrist disappears. Instead of that motion, you now control the Keiraku (meridian) on the inside of the opponent's arm with the left hand, and unbalance him when he tries to avoid being thrown.

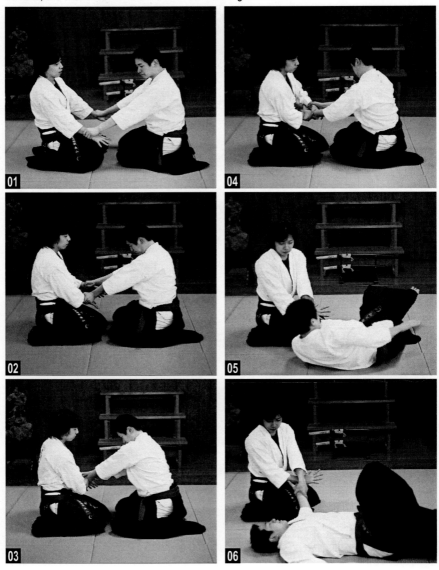

> Summary
Its sophisticated technical hierarchy and teaching system

And now Okuden Waza (ultimate high level techniques):

After repeating the process to master each technique, one after another, people finally reach the level where they can discover the most difficult techniques with a magical effect.

Hereby, several Okuden waza are introduced which are seldom shown to the public. Only through the effort of repeating these innumerable times can such techniques be realized.

photos 0-5

Ishi Datami (stone mat)
Kaiden/Okuden Waza

The opponent attacks by trying to grasp your chest with their right hand. You lead that right hand with your left hand, and his left hand with your right hand, from inside to out, to allow his arms to cross each other. You pin his left arm between his right arm and the right side of his body, then also pin his right arm using your left knee, then grasp his left hand with your left hand. Now the opponent is wholly controlled by your left leg/knee and left hand, with only a very small degree of contact.

> **Summary**
Its sophisticated technical hierarchy and teaching system

Kogan Shibori
(testicle squeezing) Kaiden/Okuden Waza

The opponent grasps both of your wrists. You move the right hand up and the left hand down by applying Gakun to the lung meridian of both wrists. Then control him by crossing both of his arms. As a result, he pins his left hand/arm with his own right arm. Then allow his right arm to go through his groin, and pull up it from behind him, which squeezes his testicles.

27

Suwari Gyaku Go Nage
(seated reversal five throw)
Kaiden/Okuden Waza

You begin from a hopeless situation as the opponent snatches up both of your wrists from behind you while seated. You should pull his hands/arms by dropping down both elbows without resisting against his grip. Next, move both hands from back to front, then throw him over your head, and control the opponent by crossing his arms (there are Kuden, or "verbal instructions" to transfer the knowledge of how to press the small intestine meridian using the small finger).

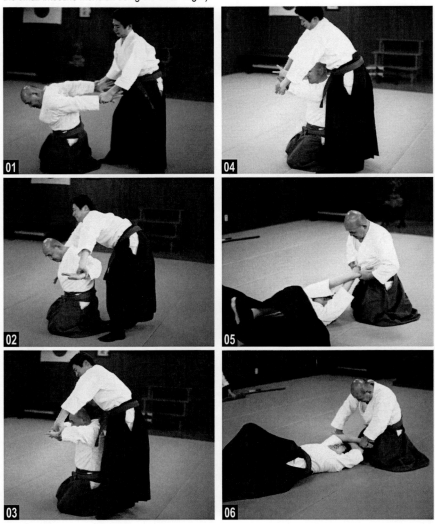

Its sophisticated technical hierarchy and teaching system

Summary

Katana Tsuka Osae Dori
(controlling the sword handle)
Kaiden/Okuden Waza

The opponent grasps the handle of your sword (tsuka) using both hands. You push down the sword so that he cannot draw the sword from its sheath due to the curvature of the blade. The opponent loses his balance because he tries to keep his grip on the handle, and you apply Gakun to his right wrist along the heart meridian. In an instant, you raise his body by applying Gakun, and strike his side using the butt-end of the handle (Tsuka Kashira). Throw him while keeping control of his wrist, then strike (Ate) the vital point (Kyusho) of his head, i.e. bile meridian, using the end of the sword handle (Tsuka Kashira).

In this technique there are multiple kime points during the sequence that give depth to the structure of this technique.

Chapter 1

To raise your hand as if to scratch your itchy ear

"In case the opponent grasps your right wrist by his left hand, you should focus your target when applying Waza onto his right foot."

In Hakkoryu there is a principle that a weak point appears where the tension occurs due to the person's putting or concentrating his force there when he tries to attack the other. And accordingly Okuyama 2nd Soke pointed out the right foot should be the place where the attacker concentrates his force in that case. But why the right foot?

"A human body does not always act as one expects" Okuyama 2nd Soke said, and grinned.

After watching his performance I could understand what he said. When I considered it the first time, I guessed the place where one concentrates force should depend on the posturing of the attacker. But after watching the actual attacking action several times I could recognize that the attacker concentrated some force onto his right foot every time.

I guess he unconsciously positioned his body on his right foot when he tried to attack by grasping 2nd Soke's right wrist with his left hand. The person who took the attacker's role never expected it and he was very surprised when this was pointed out by Okuyama 2nd Soke.

Okuyama 2nd Soke continued, "We call this phenomenon as a form of mental effect. The founder discovered how to make the most of this mental effect using Jujutsu techniques and Hakkoryu Jujutsu was founded based on that concept."

I made my goal writing this book to elucidate or disclose the secret of Hakkoryu, with the key point of this mental effect. But this mental effect itself is invisible, as such I need Okuyama 2nd Soke's detailed explanation

Chapter 1
To raise your hand as if to scratch your itchy ear

from the very basic point or I could never understand this concept. Now let's start from the beginners' level.

When the opponent grasps Okuyama 2nd Soke's right wrist with his left hand and tries to hit him with their right fist, Okuyama 2nd Soke blocks the opponent's further action by a small operation of his grasped right hand.

Okuyama 2nd Soke immediately sensed the attacker's force concentrated at his right foot and transferred his consciousness to that point through all of his body which blocks the attacker's further action. Then the opponent had stiffened their whole body and could not make further action. Okuyama 2nd Soke explained that it is important to leverage your strong intention to penetrate your conscious thought into the opponent's body.

photo 1-1

◉ Scratch your itchy ear:

Here again the consequence of Hakko Dori is shown with [photos 1-2]. At a glance it looks like a simple "releasing action of the grasped wrist". For this technique the action shown in the first 3 photos is the most important part. Unless you have never tried this yourself, you will never notice how difficult this technique is.

The action itself is quite unique, it translates to 8 movement toward the light. I suppose many of the readers might have received instruction as "If you place your arms tightly to the side of your body, then you can raise your arms." In this way one can surely create stronger physical power in their arms which helps to raise them. But in Hakkoryu, the correct way is based on a totally different theory applications.

31

"In case the opponent grasps your wrist with much stronger power than you expect, you unconsciously put your attention onto the muscle of the grasped arm. Accordingly you start trying to raise your arm with force and it does not work.

In such a case you should not put your conscious thought onto the muscle of the arm, nor onto the grasped wrist. You should wholly forget that your arm is grasped."

Although I received such instruction from Okuyama 2nd Soke, I cannot help thinking that it is still the arm's muscle which raises arm, which could already be a bad start in attempting to use this mental effect.

Then he advised me again as below.

"If you try to raise your arm using muscle, it becomes a competition of your power and the opponent's power. We should strictly avoid such situations in Hakkoryu. At first you should wholly relax yourself. Then you should create force from the Tanden (abdomen) but not from the arm."

After hearing this advice to "create force from the Tanden but not from the arm" I started feeling I could relax myself without putting force in my arm. Then forces in my body started to organize the correct correlated motion, although there should not be any special organization in my Tanden which can create force alone. Perhaps we human beings have such a mechanism that we can create force from the entire body if we become conscious to our Tanden. This also could be a kind of mental effect.

Not only in Jujutsu but also in many other Bujutsu, people place significant importance on how to leverage this organized power of the Tanden. So I noticed its importance once again. But on the other hand, I still cannot help but use the biceps muscle in my upper arm to raise my arm. But Okuyama 2nd Soke's one short instruction had solved my confusion immediately.

"Raise your arm as if you are scratching your itchy ear"

So I tried exactly as he advised me. I imagined my ear was itchy and tried to scratch that ear with my grasped hand. Then what a big surprise it was! I could raise my grasped arm easily.

Okuyama 2nd Soke explained to me further.

"People might think there exists many different and correct ways to carry out one thing. But the best way is always a single way and not several. You only have to find it and do it. Please imagine when you scratch your itchy ear,

Chapter 1
To raise your hand as if to scratch your itchy ear

Hakko Dori

photos 1-2

Start from the situation that both of your wrists are grasped and pushed downwards

First, try to raise just the right hand. Then the opponent increases his pushing force against you raising motion

Instead of competing against his pushing force, just keep performing the raising motion. The opponent cannot block your raising motion. Here, please pay attention to Okuyama 2nd Soke's relaxed arm.

Finally Okuyama 2nd Soke could raise his grasped right wrist and his freed hand goes up. He raised his hand as if he tried to scratch his itchy ear using that same hand.

you never intentionally try to find the way to move your arm or which muscle you should use."

Hearing his additional explanation, I surely agree with what he says.

"Wow, it is so simple!" I immediately understood it, but then I thought about it differently, i.e. I tried to raise my arm by putting my conscious thought onto the wrong point. Accordingly I tried to raise my arm in a wrong way.

When one tries to carry out one thing and he encounters even a tiny degree of resistance, he might fall into such a situation that he starts to resort to inappropriate reactions.

Okuyama 2nd Soke continued his explanation.

"Mental effect happens instantaneously and accordingly, unconsciously. That is why it might cause inappropriate reactions. It might happen in such a case that you cannot raise your arm because the opponent grasps your wrist with stronger force than your expectation. At the instant you feel it, you start thinking you have to create stronger force in your arm. Such simple thinking of comparing force triggers putting force into the muscles of your arm. Then you stop thinking over the other possibilities and that idea leads you to the worst scenario. You should imagine that your arm was free from the grasp and you could move it freely. I advise you to try to move your hand/arm as if you are scratching your itchy ear using that hand. This means you move your arm as if your arm was free."

In most Bujutsu and competition sports, people try their best to attain the strength by which they can overcome their opponent and/or target. I believe they put their greatest effort to attain that goal. On the contrary, we aim for a totally different goal in Hakkoryu. Generally speaking, in Bujutsu one can never compete with the same opponent twice. The competition would be just once which results in winning (live) or losing (death) and the competition with the same opponent can never occur again. Accordingly if you lost a single match, there is no next chance for you to prepare and improve.

Then what should you do in Bujutsu?

You only have to take the most appropriate motion in a natural way. The problem often occurs in the moment you get the idea that you still have a chance for a rematch if you cannot win this time. It happens instantaneously and unconsciously.

Chapter 1
To raise your hand as if to scratch your itchy ear

Besides, one tends to consider that it is a natural reaction for one to think over the rematch in the case of losing that first match and it causes the biggest problem.

"If you fail to raise your arm, then you try to increase your force." You should notice that this is the wrong way of thinking from the start.

◉ Hakkoryu's three main principles: no challenge, no resistance and no injury

"When I receive a guest for their first trial class at our Dojo, I can immediately distinguish the person's intention when I let him perform Hakko Dori and he grasps my wrists. His intention can be to compete with me or to learn from me, or both, which means he has not decided yet. I often encounter such situations, especially abroad where there are so many men with strong muscles who try to challenge and defeat me by creating a situation in which I cannot raise my hand in Hakko Dori. In such a situation I should never try to compete with them using power. If I do so I cannot raise my grasped arms. It is our principle that you become weaker as you try to compete with the opponent by increasing your power."

In Hakkoryu they put their highest value on the obedient personality of the Deshi (student). In other words, they have the three main principles: no challenge, no resistance and no injury. These three restrictions explain how we should deal with mental effect which is caused automatically and instantaneously in many cases. Unnecessary reactions such as intimidation, bravado, bullying, weakness, and so on are caused in the certain cases. I might suggest that those negative elements which lead a person to failure, not only in Bujutsu, but also in everyday life are caused by this mental effect.

When you are faced with a difficult task, you probably carry it out by forgetting all those negative mental attitudes and just simply do it, like raising your arm just simply to scratch your itchy ear.

This is Hakkoryu's concept, how to deal with mental effect teaches us how we should behave in the difficult situations. That concept teaches us to never worry, which is not necessary at all.

"It could be difficult to realize that concept. But I can explain to you in easier words, such as "Change your mind and never stick to one idea".

The process of how negative mental effect occurs instantaneously

When your wrist is grasped and you try to raise that grasped arm, you might feel in the forehand that you probably cannot raise your hand due to the opponent's strong force. Then, as a natural reaction, you put more force into the muscles of your arm immediately and unconsciously. Accordingly you only let the biceps muscle in your upper arm work and it blocks the ability to create co-organized action thorough all of your body. It is quite difficult to take the most proper action in any given situation. It is the know-how of trying to scratch the itchy ear which allows you to notice the most proper action to take.

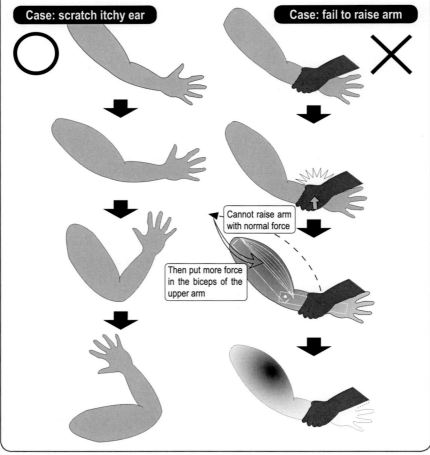

illustration 1-1

Chapter 1
To raise your hand as if to scratch your itchy ear

Anyway it is important not to think it over too much."
Okuyama 2nd Soke gave this further advice to me and laughed loudly.

Hearing his additional advice above, I started accepting his idea and I started wishing I could do so. I also started laughing together with Okuyama 2nd Soke.

I must confess that I am the type of person who is often lost in thought, but at that moment, I could accept his concept quite naturally and easily. It was the instant that I could feel myself a little more grown up.

I started writing this book with a subject of mental effect which has an enormous amount of related topics and subject matters. Those will be explained in greater detail later. By the way, it is just one of the examples of how to explain the huge related subjects that the founder wrote a book titled "analogical hitting mark method" which could be applied to gambling such as horse racing.

Chapter 2

Imagine yourself as a great Buddha statue

◈ Never try to forcefully lower your grip if you actually want to lower it.

In Chapter 1, we focused on the raising arm motion and in this chapter we focus on lowering the arm as an opposite motion. Please remember it is important not to use force for the raising arm motion. In other words, it is important to avoid partial muscle operation which tends to occur unconsciously. This is the biggest basic concept that is commonly applied to all the movements in Hakkoryu.

Everybody reading this might suppose that it should be quite difficult to realize this concept. But Okuyama 2nd Soke says "Normally, it could be the easiest way because you just simply can do it quite naturally."

It is still very difficult for me to realize this basic concept, which means I probably do not do it naturally according to Okuyama 2nd Soke's explanation. Regardless, this lowering arm motion seems easier than the raising arm motion, in my opinion.

"Of course everybody understands that it does not require force just to lower their free arm. But when you execute an actual technique with this motion it is not so easy anymore."

Okuyama 2nd Soke showed me a part of Uchi Komi Dori as an example which is shown in the photos on [photos 2-1], no.1 shows the phase that Okuyama 2nd Soke blocks the opponent's strike with his right hand and holds his right fist with his right hand and wrist by his left hand. Then he starts lowering his two hands to make Kuzushi (unbalancing) to the opponent.

This sequence is similar to both Nikajo Kime in Daitoryu and Nikyo in

Chapter 2
Imagine yourself as a great Buddha statue

Aikido. Also there is a similar technique in Kinki Jutsu which originated in China. They also show this technique very often with photos and those photos give an impression that the attacker receives a sharp pain in his grasped wrist by the defender's vertical bending motion using both hands. And due to that pain the attacker is forced to fall on his knees. Based on that idea most of people try to bend the attacker's wrist vertically using both hands to force the attacker on his knees.

In such a motion you can use only your wrists which cannot produce enough force. Then you try to use force in your arms to make the attacker kneel. In such a case you can leverage using only the triceps muscle in your upper arms (muscle attached to backside of your upper arm). The force produced in both cases is still insufficient to succeed.

It is the wrong way if you try to control the opponent's wrist or to force him down intentionally, because these actions unconsciously cause local muscle operation which was described at the beginning of this chapter.

"It is not by force that you should perform this action. It is no use to try to leverage force created by wrists or by arms. You should transfer your entire body weight onto the grasping point, i.e. the attacker's grasped wrist. You make your entire body weight as one block of mass. Then you can finally unbalance the attacker."

But it is still quite difficult to perform it properly. If you are told as above, you surely have the idea that you should put your body weight onto the opponent's wrist from above, or you should try to "hang" your bodyweight on his wrist. Such acts mean just putting static mass on the opponent and no more. It creates no movement, nor motion. In Bujutsu, it has a different meaning to say "put your whole body weight". This instruction has a completely different action.

"If I instruct someone to integrate their body, then in most cases he makes a part of his body stiff. But in reality it can be possible to integrate one's body only by relaxing the whole body. In Hakkoryu, we instruct students to imagine themselves as a huge Buddha statue."

Just imagine a huge Buddha statue. It has great mass, but there is no force concentrated in any single part of its structure. Its whole structure consists of uniform material. There is no unevenness, nor deviation. If you imagine that you became a huge Buddha statue, there appears to be no force concentrating

The stronger you try to lower your grip the harder it becomes to do.

Photo No.1 on [photos 2-1] shows the action to execute Kime on the opponent's wrist. You can find a similar technique called Nikajo Kime in Daito-ryu. In this case you put the opponent's hand on your chest tightly, then you can bend the opponent's wrist rather easily. You can find a similar technique in most Koryu Jujutsu, as an example, Hikiotoshi in Asayama Ichiden-ryu Jujutsu. But in this technique, the hand is held away from your chest, it becomes more difficult to do it than it appears. Then you tend to bend the opponent wrist vertically using the force of both of your hands. -> Figure-1

As the next option, you tend to pull that hand down by using force in the biceps muscles of your upper arms. -> Fig-2   In each case you can just use the force created by the wrists or biceps muscle in your upper arms, which is not sufficient to realize the result you intend to get. If you try to lower your gripping hands more forcefully, this results in a smaller action because only part of your body shall be engaged in the operation. In such a case you had better do nothing. In Hakkoryu, they teach you to become a huge Buddha statue. By imaging this, you can integrate your whole body in one mass.

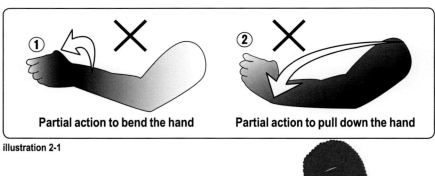

illustration 2-1

By forming a mental image to try to become a huge Buddha statue, your whole body is integrated in one. If you simply try to integrate your whole body consciously then you tend to get stiff in some place within your body. You can avoid such a situation by imagining becoming a huge Buddha statue. A huge Buddha statue does not move. It is calm and stable. That is why it is so fine. As shown in [photos 2-1], no.3, it is by using body weight, not force, by which Okuyama 2nd Soke unbalances the opponent.

Chapter 2
Imagine yourself as a great Buddha statue

Uchi Komi Dori

photos 2-1

Okuyama 2nd Soke catches the opponent's right fist using his right hand and holds their wrist with his left hand. Then Okuyama 2nd Soke starts unbalancing him.

Here you tend to bend the opponent's wrist vertically to execute Kime on his wrist, but it does not work. And then you tend to pull down the opponent's hand, which does not work neither.

Here Okuyama 2nd Soke transfers his body weight via the path of the opponent's wrist ->lower arm -> elbow -> upper arm -> shoulder -> trunk, by centimeters, in a very natural motion. The opponent cannot resist because he receives Okuyama 2nd Soke's full body weight but not the force of just his hands and arms.

in your body. It must be an excellent idea to make such an image to become a huge Buddha statue.

"You will fail if you try to lower your grip only using force in arms. But by making such an image in your mind that your entire weight will be transferred into the opponent's body through the point of contact, i.e. your grip and the opponent's wrist, such weight transfer can be done successfully as a result of the mental effect, not by the application of physical force."

During this weight transfer, Okuyama 2nd Soke explains, "Now my weight reaches the opponent's wrist." "Now it goes to his elbow." "Now it reaches his shoulder, then it goes into his body." He describes the process of how his body weight penetrates into the opponent's entire body. In fact the opponent feels less freedom to move the deeper Okuyama 2nd Soke's body weight penetrates through his body. In the end, he became totally unbalanced and fell down on the floor.

"I can control my weight transfer by centimeters. That is the clear difference between body weight transfer and force application. With force, even if it is immense, you can only apply it just to bend the opponent's wrist. Even if the force applied is stronger, you can bend the opponent's wrist stronger and nothing more. Hakkoryu's techniques are not leveraging of such simple physical force applications.

◈ Pain increases pain

According to the uncertainty principle of quantum mechanics theory, if you put light on an extremely tiny substance such as the size of an atom in order to observe it, it changes its characteristics as a result of being illuminated. If you want to continue to observe it, it will change characteristics even more and accordingly, you can never observe that substance as it is in that very instance. I now feel similar weariness that if I lower my arm stronger, the action becomes more difficult.

"It is important where you put your consciousness. Let me try this…….." with that, Okuyama 2nd Soke put his sharp bent middle finger joint to his student's chest, around the sternum, against a weak point called the Danchu, and pushed it. (refer to [photos 2-2], the first part). Of course, the opponent distorted his face as the result of sharp penetrating pain. That is the place

Chapter 2
Imagine yourself as a great Buddha statue

between the left and right pectoral muscles which is covered by thin skin and directly connected to the bone, one of the weak points. He could not bear such pain.

Then changing offence and defense, the opponent pushed Okuyama 2nd Soke at the same place in exactly same way as Okuyama 2nd Soke did. But Okuyama 2nd Soke seemed to receive no pain. On the contrary, he pushed the opponent back, even as he continued to apply pressure against his chest. (refer to [photos 2-2], the latter part)

"You should focus your consciousness here (the place the opponent puts his sharp finger joint). But you still should not apply unnecessary force here. Then you will not feel pain, but the opponent starts feeling he is being pushed back. You have to do this while concentrating your conscious thought so strongly that the weak point will disappear."

It is very difficult. You should concentrate your consciousness but never create tension at the point.

"Tension is created when you are fearful or you react sharply against even a small amount of pain. And it causes the weak point to be even more sensitive."

When you feel pain, the body reacts to it unconsciously, i.e. automatically. Against this natural reaction of the human body, you should train yourself so that you can keep this tension-free condition. This is a very important concept in Hakkoryu.

As you try to do some action with a stronger intention, you might fall into a situation where you find it much more difficult. The theme of this chapter seems to become a frustrating paradox. Then a question came to me. "If this is the case, could I do it better if I try with weaker intention? Of course it cannot be so. The answer is clear.

If you have become too hot to do something, you cannot always achieve the expected good result. Because in such a situation you might miss your goal and keep going forward without knowing where the goal is.

Such things might often happen for human beings that a person becomes too serious, becomes combative, or feels a sense of fear by anticipating their failure. All those acts happen quite naturally for human beings. But even in such situations, if you can calm yourself and observe what is happening around you with a stable mind, the situation is seen quite differently.

I guess Hakkoryu is a Bujutsu system which guides you to such ideal situations.

Anyway, I begin to think over again that a mind and consciousness, which is the theme of this book, are quite difficult themes to be understood correctly and properly. I remember what Okuyama 2nd Soke said. "Concentrate your mind, but never concentrate on physical force"

What do the readers think about this theme?

As far as I'm concerned, in most of the cases I become anxious when I attempt to concentrate my conscious thought, or intent. Does it mean I concentrate my consciousness in the wrong way?

I asked Okuyama 2nd Soke what he means by "concentration" and how and what I should concentrate on.

"Well it is too difficult to explain that concept clearly at this stage. So I will explain it in plain words, step by step."

photos 2-2

Your body's reaction to

Okuyama 2nd Soke put his sharp bent middle finger joint onto the opponent's chest, around the sternum, which covered by thin flesh. He should feel sharp and unbearably strong pain.

Chapter 2
Imagine yourself as a great Buddha statue

feel pain makes your body more sensitive to pain

Now the opponent does the same action to Okuyama 2nd Soke but Okuyama 2nd Soke feels no pain and Okuyama 2nd Soke starts pushing his student back to unbalance him. This is not because Okuyama 2nd Soke is extraordinary. Okuyama 2nd Soke says, "If you can relax your body, you do not feel pain at all." It is easy to say this, but difficult to do. Because that place is covered only by a thin layer of flesh and accordingly, is a weak point. Even a small push could cause enormous pain. Your natural reaction to tense up there for protection causes your body to become more pain sensitive.

This tension and straining could be created even before the sharp bent finger joint touches one's chest because of the fear associated with the anticipation of receiving it. That is awkward. You really need to have a stable mind which does not make such overreactions. Well, that is why you have to create the mental image of a huge Buddha statue to avoid such overreaction.

45

Chapter 3

Do not resist, then you can realize the techniques

◈ Unfathomable depth of Kaiden Waza (highest level technique)

Two strange mechanisms of the human body were introduced both in Chapter 1 as arm raising motion and in Chapter 2 as arm lowering motion. Both motions could be performed by unmeasurable "strength", which is created as a result of eliminating one's conscious thought to raise or to lower the arm.

In this chapter we focus on those motions from a different perspective. In the previous chapters we focused on the defender's body movements but now we focus on the mechanics of the opponent's body. Please watch the technique that Okuyama 2nd Soke showed in the photos on the next page. The opponent has grasped Okuyama 2nd Soke's right wrist with his right hand and tried to strike Okuyama 2nd Soke's face with his left fist. But at that moment, his next action was blocked, and he could do no further action. This same technique I introduced briefly in Chapter 1, but now Okuyama 2nd Soke's movement has become much smaller. It even seemed as though he made no movement himself.

In the next case the opponent grasped both of Okuyama 2nd Soke's wrists and tried to kick him. In the same way he was completely blocked and could not kick Okuyama 2nd Soke, [photos 3-1].

"It is not by the controlling or locking (Kime) of his wrists that I blocked his action"

What Okuyama 2nd Soke said is apparent, because Okuyama 2nd Soke did almost nothing against the opponent's attack.

"Hakkoryu techniques are categorized into three levels as Ippan Waza

Chapter 3
Do not resist, then you can realize the techniques

photos 3-1

The opponent's movement is blocked/controlled by the intention that one does not resist against his attack.

The three photos at left show that further movement of the opponent was blocked when he grasped Okuyama 2nd Soke's left wrist and tried to hit him with his left fist. The three photos of the right show the opponent's further movement to kick Okuyama 2nd Soke was blocked after grasping both his wrists.

(general level techniques), Shihan Waza (instructor's level techniques) and Kaiden Waza (highest level techniques). Those two techniques which I showed here are categorized as Kaiden Waza. I never teach those two techniques to Shihan level students." said Okuyama 2nd Soke.

"Whoops! These are such high level techniques. Then I should listen to what Okuyama 2nd Soke says with full of my attention."

"2nd Soke, what are you doing then? Why could the opponent not hit or kick you?" I asked Okuyama 2nd Soke. "You do not need to ask me with such hesitation. But, it is quite difficult to explain what happened through words. I would like to explain this phenomenon in an easier way so that even people who have no experience in Hakkoryu might understand.

It is important not to create tension in yourself, which makes a person very weak. In Hakkoryu we say that you shall be defeated if you create tension in yourself."

I can understand what he says because I already experienced this concept in the previous Chapters 1 and 2. When you become tense, your body becomes stiff and you lose freedom of your body's movement. If your body becomes stiff, it is easy for your opponent to apply techniques on you, which is logical. But it is not restricted only for those cases in which you try to do something using force that your body becomes stiff and immobile. Such tension and stiffness in the body also happens when one feels fear. Especially for such a case as the attacker grasps both of your wrists and will kick you, then you became tense through a sensation of fear. If this were to happen to me, I would surely become strained and tense terribly by a strong sense of fear.

"For such a case, you really need to be calm and to keep a stable mind. It seems that a person should be strictly disciplined and trained to be able to behave this way in such a situation. But you can realize this mental state much easier if you abandon in your own mind, the thought of resisting against your opponent's attacking action."

Well, in such a case where you do not resist, then you do not have to fear because the opponent cannot be your enemy any longer. Of course, it is not so easy to do it as Okuyama 2nd Soke said.

"Also, in these cases you should not take different actions according to the different ways the opponent attacks you, such as, if he tries to hit you

Chapter 3
Do not resist, then you can realize the techniques

Attacking action can be performed only if the other reacts.

There is no need to say that an attacking action can only be performed if there is an object to attack. We also can say that the attack can only be performed if the other reacts against that attacking action. Attacking action can be performed if the other tries to resist or avoid it and the attacker can fine tune or alter his attacking action according to those reactions.

That is the reason an attacker cannot continue to execute his attacking action to the object who does not resist. Okuyama 2nd Soke's action went even further than a "no resisting situation", where he integrated, or connected himself to the opponent's body to paralyze him and as a result, Okuyama 2nd Soke blocked the opponent's movement.

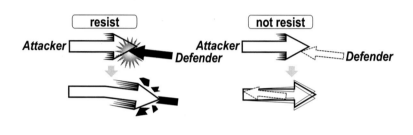

illustration 3-1

with his left hand then you block by…. or if he tries to kick using his right foot then you block by ….. You must notice what reaction you should take through your sensitivity, and accordingly you should be able to do it even with your eyes closed."

Now I can finally guess what happened. Because Okuyama 2nd Soke made no resisting behavior, like not trying to avoid nor resist against the opponent's attacking action. He probably integrated himself to the opponent in his mind. Then I suddenly noticed the fact that it was because of Okuyama 2nd Soke's mental sensitivity to the opponent that he fell into the state where he could not hit nor kick Okuyama 2nd Soke, "Yes, it should be such a feeling. In fact the attacker needs to receive some reaction from his object when the person attacks that object. Without this reaction, an attacking action cannot be practically done."

I now began to deeply understand the reason why the opponent stopped his attack. The opponent anticipates the other's reaction, such as resistance or avoiding when he makes the attacking action. If such reaction does not happen, the opponent cannot carry out his attack. If the other does not resist, the opponent cannot execute his attack and he becomes unconsciously joined by the other person. As a result his whole body has been controlled by some kind of paralysis. This is exactly the case that happened.

"It might happen that some stranger suddenly attacks you when he is passing by you. You normally cannot react against such a sudden attack with good timing, and your reaction shall occur too late. That is why you have to always behave with the precondition to not resist against such an attack in the first place. Only in such a "weaker" situation, can you apply techniques to the attacker. That is Hakkoryu's concept. And that is why it works against even a very strong opponent.

◈ Paralyzing

"It does not matter for you how strong the opponent is." Such an ideal situation that is every martial artists dream really does exist. If one can say "it does not matter" with great confidence, he does not even need to, nor intend to resist against the attack.

The meaning of this mental effect is quite deep.

But anyway it seems like quite a strange technique, even after you understand the theory of how it works. As you can see, there is nothing physical actually blocking the opponent by which he was totally stopped from further action. "Is it because of pain that he could not move?" I asked Okuyama 2nd Soke. Because giving pain is the specialty of Hakkoryu.

"No, it is not by pain that he was blocked. He became wholly paralyzed and he was not controlled by pain. Pain only occurs in him simply as a result, not as a tool through which to paralyze him."

Then Okuyama 2nd Soke showed me another Kaiden Waza as presented on the next page. Okuyama 2nd Soke was captured by the opponent by both wrists from behind. Then in a moment he reversed positions with the opponent. It is normally impossible for anybody to resist against the pulling arm power of the opponent from behind, unless he has much stronger power in his arms than the opponent.

Chapter 3
Do not resist, then you can realize the techniques

Okuyama 2nd Soke might guide the opponent because he does not resist against the opponent's power. Here we should pay particular attention to how the posturing is at the end of the sequence. The opponent cannot release his grasping hands and has to keep holding Okuyama 2nd Soke by both of his wrists, which causes the situation where he clinches himself with his own arms. Accordingly, he cannot escape from this painful posture by himself and is locked in place.

"In this case, I never specifically intend to apply a technique to him."

It might be a result in such a case where the opponent attacks a person who does not resist. Okuyama 2nd Soke's movement looks so normal and not special at all, but on the contrary, the result is miraculous, which even frightened me.

After all this, I reconsidered the meaning of this chapter's theme: "no resistance". For me "no resistance" means to follow the other's movement and as such, I even actively try to follow it; this how I first understood Okuyama 2nd Soke's explanation. As a result there is an inconsistency between the correct meaning and what I understood. If I watch Okuyama 2nd Soke's motion, I can never find even a tiny intention to follow the attacker's movement. So, I totally misunderstood what he explained as "no resistance".

Of course it is clear that there exists no Bujutsu without some use of intention. It is the same as there is no human life without one's will to live. But it seems like people tend to misunderstand the meaning of one's will in his life, the same way they misunderstand "no resistance". People often struggle in vain, and create stress in themselves for nothing.

photos 3-2

Kaiden Waza: Tachi Gyaku Go Katame

Okuyama 2nd Soke, who has both of his wrists grasped from behind, guided the opponent to his front. This motion is done quite smoothly without any pause. Okuyama 2nd Soke can perform this motion because he does not resist against the opponent's power. As a result of this movement the opponent loses his balance. In the end, the opponent is wholly controlled by Okuyama 2nd Soke through the way he clinches himself by both of his own arms. He cannot release his grasping hands and has to keep grasping both Okuyama 2nd Soke's wrists which causes him to lose freedom of his arms and those arms are then used by Okuyama 2nd Soke to pin or hold the opponent in place.

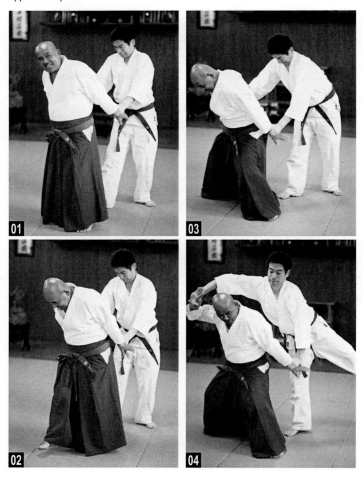

Chapter 3
Do not resist, then you can realize the techniques

(Standing Reverse Five Hold)

The photo 08 shows the final position where Okuyama 2nd Soke controls the opponent by his own two arms. Even in this situation the opponent keeps grasping both of Okuyama 2nd Soke's wrists with his own intention and power, which looks quite strange and magical.

Also shown in photo 08, the opponent's face has turned red because of this difficult posturing from which he cannot escape or let go with his hands. That said, if he could have released both his grasping hands, he could very easily have escaped from this control.

Chapter 4

Do nothing except drop yourself with gravity

◈ How you can escape from a crisis situation?

Nowadays the need for Goshin Jutsu (self-defense, or self-protection martial arts) have been increasing in the context of rising crime rates and insecurity in society. When people seek to choose a particular self-defense art to master, the question always comes to their mind, "Is this Goshin Jutsu really useful or practical for a real crisis situation?"

There is a point by which you can utilize to distinguish if it is useful or not, and that point can be applied not only to Goshin Jutsu, but also to Budo in general, as well as the other fighting sports.

The point is, whether you can take a proper action smoothly in a sudden crisis situation with the help of that particular martial art. I can explain it even more plainly as, will you be free from becoming tense and paralyzed by stiffness in such sudden life or death situations with the help of a particular martial art.

"It is our principle in Hakkoryu that we should never be tense. You should not become tense or strain yourself in any situation." said Okuyama 2nd Soke. Although I understand what Okuyama 2nd Soke means by those words, I cannot help but think that human beings surely and instantly make themselves tense when they suddenly get involved in a life or death situation. Then what can we do? Is there anything we can do to avoid being paralyzed in such situations?

"We keep practicing our techniques every day for that purpose. There is specific knowledge, although it is not easy to master it. At first, you should clearly recognise the fact that there is no need to resist such an attack."

If you are suddenly attacked by a stranger, at that instant you sense

Chapter 4
Do nothing except drop yourself with gravity

immediately "Oh, this is terrible!" Most probably, as a result, you have developed tension in your body. On the contrary, if you could accept the case as "Not so terrible at all", or in other words, if you could recognize in yourself "No need to worry, I can handle this situation. No problem." you would never become tense or strained in such a situation.

It is still not easy to recognize or accept the situation in such a way, but the result might be a lot different in such a case if you can acknowledge that resisting is not the best reaction.

"For example, if a lady was embraced from behind by a stranger, she tries to resist and to release herself from that embrace, even though she realizes it is no use because of the strong constricting force she feels against her. But in fact, there is a way she can escape from that bear hug much more easily."

The lady hugged from behind should try to expand her arms by moving her hands away from both sides of her body. During this expansion, her upper arms can only move a little compared with her lower arms, and accordingly, the clearance which she can make between hers upper arms and the stranger's tightening arms is so slight that she cannot release herself from the attacker's tightening arms/hands in a normal way of attempting to escape. However, as stated, her lower arms are free to move quite a lot. Then the lady drops her bodyweight unconsciously, which results in her being able to escape from the hug quite easily (refer to [photos 4-1]).

"If you can create a small clearance between you and the attacker, then you just drop your body. Never make your body tense and never resist the attackers tightening power. You simply create a mental image of just dropping your entire relaxed bodyweight. If you try to resist, you make your body tense, and you are immediately controlled and it is too late. You cannot do anything at that stage. That is the end."

Of course you do not need power to drop yourself. It is easy, just release all of the power and tension from your entire body and allow the weight of your body to be held in the attacker's arms. Yes, you may be able to do this in a sudden crisis situation.

On the other hand, I doubt if it is really effective to simply release all the tension and stiffness in your body during such an emergency situation. It looks like you give up all effort to escape and subsequently, you have no hope of doing so. Although Okuyama 2nd Soke instructs that we should not resist, and we should give up all our power, it must make the situation even worse by doing this, right?

Very frankly speaking, I still cannot believe the effect of this "totally abandoning power from your body" in a crisis situation.

photos 4-1

It is very easy to drop yourself.

A lady was embraced tightly from behind. After opening her arms she abandoned the force in her entire body and dropped herself. She succeeded in escaping from the hug. You do not need to think over what you should do according to the different attacking patters. It is so easy to just drop yourself. And this simplicity makes the technique quite practical in a real situation.

◈ Strength of dropping motion

For instance, if you are pulled with your hand/arm by a strong force, you first estimate if you can compete with that force using strength or counter weight. You try to convince yourself that you have to pull back on the opponent to avoid your body's unwilling displacement. And, although you resist that force, your body is moved if that force is stronger than your own counter force. It is because your force was less than the opponent's force. It is a simple power comparison, like stronger vs. weaker.

Chapter 4
Do nothing except drop yourself with gravity

If you are confident that your power is stronger than the attacker's, you resist the opponent's pulling power and will pull him back. But if his weight is heavier than yours, your body is moved toward the opponent by your own pulling. This is a basic theory of physics.

Yes, indeed, I understand that logic. But then, is there no way to compete with the stronger force or heavier weight by physical means? Because it is not easy to increase my own weight substantially, so I need a solution.

"You should only have to give up all the force and tension within your body and leave your relaxed body to the attacker's arms. You do not strain yourself and just drop your body naturally with the aid of gravity. That's it."

Okuyama 2nd Soke said "That's it." But afterwards I watched the phenomenon which was not purely as simple as "That's it", but something much more. So I started wondering even more about what he said.

When a lady was grasped by the left wrist of her straightened dainty left arm, she was pulled by the opponent—a man who is much stronger and

photos 4-2

Just drop your arm to avoid being pulled

At first you should leave your grasped arm as it is in the opponent's hand, to avoid from being pulled. Then, by using gravity, you drop your shoulder and elbow which creates tremendous power to pull the opponent to your own side.

57

heavier than herself. (Please refer to [photos 4-2].)

The lady is so slight that a normal man can lift her up very easily. Of course, one's weight cannot always be estimated properly only by looking; however, it should be apparent that she cannot defeat this man's strong power using her small arm alone.

It is surely not power that is generated by muscular strength that she used in this case. She just let her arm drop by gravity. How could such a simple motion create such strong force? Besides, did she even create power by dropping her arm?

"If you abandon strength from your horizontally outstretched arm, it drops naturally. The motion is just that. It is an everyday motion and nothing more. The simplest motion, without inefficiency, can be the strongest motion."

The reaction you should take in the situation that you are pulled is not to pull back, but to just leave your arm to the opponent's grasp, then drop it. That is very easy. In other words, you can describe it as "do nothing".

In fact, do you think you can easily pull a rope whose end is bound to 40 kg's of weight (about 90lbs)?

The answer is "no". If a women with 40kg's of mass can relax herself, have no tension in her body, and leaves her entire body to the force of gravity, it creates a much stronger force than you can imagine. It is exactly the same situation as above.

It is very practical instruction to try to drop yourself using gravity. Here, mental effect should also be involved.

If it was the case that you should raise your body up instead of sink it down, then you surely would create tension in your body and make it stiff because you cannot use the help of gravity in this case.

In Hakkoryu, people are always guided to the easier solution because it is more natural, and accordingly, more effective as a technique. You only have to apply your everyday motion, which means exactly that.

In Hakkoryu, it is much more important to practise polite bowing and arm lowering in a smooth way, without useless movement, than it is to continue simple pattern training. Here pattern training means, if the opponent attacks in that way, you should react in this way, etc., which is based on various way of reacting.

Chapter 4
Do nothing except drop yourself with gravity

At first, I thought all those techniques were impossible to perform using the laws of physics, but on the contrary, they are surely based on it. This I discovered, although the applicable laws used are not easily recognized in every case.

◈ The techniques applicable in any situation

In Hakkoryu, you find a lot of similar techniques which begin with the situation in which your wrist is grasped. We now try to overlook what was done during the procedures introduced up until now, because those were done so smoothly and naturally that I could not understand them well. But now, I can recognise them by watching these techniques and hearing Okuyama 2nd Soke's explanation.

Then, Okuyama 2nd Soke showed me the two similar techniques which start in the same way as one is grasped by his wrist (refer to [photos 4-3]).

Shodan-Gi (1st Dan level) Yoko Katate Osae Dori

The opponent approaches Okuyama 2nd Soke who is seated. He grasps Okuyama 2nd Soke's right wrist with his left hand and tries to pull it towards him. Okuyama 2nd Soke immediately moves close to the opponent using Shikkou (walking on knees) to avoid being pulled towards him. By this first action, Okuyama 2nd Soke avoided becoming unbalanced through the opponent's pulling. This is the very basic and important starting point.

Sandan-Gi (3rd Dan level) Yoko Dori

This technique starts with the same situation as the previous one. Okuyama 2nd Soke unbalances the opponent, who has taken a much stronger posture than Okuyama 2nd Soke, by pulling him toward Okuyama 2nd Soke. Of course, it is not done by force in the arm, but through the motion of "dropping the arm by gravity" that Okuyama 2nd Soke uses here.

Many of the Hakkoryu techniques look miraculous, not like cheap decoration, and one cannot easily reach a level of mastery where they can execute those miraculous techniques easily.

Besides, from its origin, Hakkoryu has been specialized in self-defense.

59

So in principle, all its techniques should able to be mastered and performed by everyone. If you consider this chapter's theme to be "do nothing except just drop yourself with gravity", you should find it quite interesting.

When it comes to Goshin Jutsu, the question of "if it is applicable or not for a real life or death situation", which is described in the beginning of this chapter, should be quite an important point to be considered.

One way is to compile many self-defense patters which are related to the different ways of being attacked in various hypothetical situations. But it

The two techniques, both start from the situation that one wrist is grasped from your side and pulled. It will be too late if your body is completely moved and accordingly, unbalanced by the pulling motion. So, you have to react immediately to avoid being completely pulled away. Let's start with Shodan-Gi, Yoko Katate Osae Dori. In this case Okuyama 2nd

photos 4-3

Shodan-Gi (1st Dan level)
Yoko Katate Osae Dori

As Okuyama 2nd Soke is sitting, the standing opponent approaches him and grasps his right wrist with the left hand. At that moment the opponent tries to pull Okuyama 2nd Soke's right wrist, while Okuyama 2nd Soke opens his grasped wrist fully in "Hakko", at the same time he is moving his body close to the opponent using Shikkuo. Then, he grasps

the back of the opponent's left wrist using his left hand. Okuyama 2nd Soke raises both hands, which creates a wrist lock to unbalance the opponent. Okuyama 2nd Soke then rotates the locked wrist clockwise over his head to guide the opponent around behind him. At the end of this rotation, Okuyama 2nd Soke releases his grasped right wrist from the opponent's left hand, but maintains his control of the opponent's left wrist with his left hand, he throws the opponent onto the floor by pulling his left hand down.

Chapter 4
Do nothing except drop yourself with gravity

should be far more practical to remember only one basic concept, such as "do nothing except just drop yourself with gravity" than it is to remember all those different self-defense patterns, and to choose the best one from among them in an instant.

In any case, if you can prevent yourself from being unbalanced by the opponent's pulling motion, it is much easier for you to continue to escape from the crisis situation. It is very easy to just drop your body, or body parts, with the effect of gravity because it is a natural motion.

Soke moved his body close to the opponent using Shikko to avoid being pulled away by him. On the other hand, in the next technique from Sandan-Gi (Yoko Dori), Okuyama 2nd Soke pulls the opponent back and unbalances him without himself moving. The action "do nothing except just drop your arm" enables this action.

Sandan-Gi (3rd Dan level)
Yoko Dori

As Okuyama 2nd Soke is sitting, the standing opponent approaches him and grasps his left wrist with the right hand. At that moment the opponent tries to pull Okuyama 2nd Soke's left wrist, Okuyama 2nd Soke leaves his grasped arm in the opponent's hand and just drops down his own arm, which results in pulling the opponent's body to him. Okuyama 2nd Soke then rotates the grasped left arm/wrist from out to in, which creates a lock on the opponent's right wrist, then Okuyama 2nd Soke applies downward pressure on the lock to force the opponent down. After throwing, Okuyama 2nd Soke presses the opponent's right shoulder using his left knee as the final control.

Chapter 5

Open my hand in the Hakko shape

◈ When to be conscious so that you can be unconscious

In Hakkoryu you are instructed to open your hand into the shape of Hakko (eighth light), in case your wrist is grasped. And there might be some misunderstanding in how people interpret the meaning of this Hakko shape.

People might tend to think that they visualise the Hakko shape as the light spreading into all directions (meaning eight-directions). Accordingly, they try to stretch all the five fingers as much as possible, as light spreads out and emanates. Although I have interviewed Okuyama 2nd Soke several times already, I also thought this was the case until now.

"One needs to put force in his hand to make such a light diffusion pattern (shape) and it is not good, as you see now. It is our basic principle not to put force—not only in your hand—but also in your whole body. You should open your hand by lightly stretching all fingers with uniform distance

photos 5-1

In Hakkoryu you are instructed to open your hand into the shape of Hakko (eighth light) in the case that your wrist is grasped. This is the basic action of Hakkoryu.

Chapter 5
Open my hand in the Hakko shape

between each in a natural way. This is the exact meaning of how to open your hand in the Hakko shape.

Now I understood the correct meaning of opening the hand in the Hakko shape. In fact, light spreads uniformly without deviation. A hand has a lot of freedom of movement, and accordingly, it is hard to lose its force uniformly. Or, on the contrary, if all fingers were not stretched out uniformly, you could not use force correctly in your hand.

Well, now let's consider again what it means to open the hand in the Hakko shape. As I mentioned already, at first I thought it meant to open the hand with fully and forcefully stretched out fingers. But this is not the case. Then what should be the case....?

"For instance, if your wrist is grasped and you want to move that arm, it is very hard to do it using power. In other words, if you focus your consciousness on the point where you are grasped (in this case your wrist) you cannot help putting force on that place."

In the previous Chapter 1, Okuyama 2nd Soke introduced a way "to scratch your itchy ear" as to raise one's arm without being conscious of your grasped wrist.

"In fact, I already performed this method of opening my hand in the Hakko shape when I demonstrated Hakko Dori. It is quite useful to open your hand without conscious action, so you can avoid thinking about the place where you have been grabbed. If a person consciously puts force on that point, he automatically holds his hand in the shape of a fist. That is why

photos 5-2

In Chapter 1, Okuyama, 2nd Soke, introduced Hakko Dori as a way to "scratch your itchy ear", or to raise one's arm without being conscious of your grasped wrist. This is the concept of how to shift one's consciousness away from the wrist that is grasped by trying to scratch your itchy ear.

it is most effective to try not holding a fist by this simple physical motion. Of course it might be possible not to put force into the place where you are grabbed, or while making a fist, or vice versa, as a Kata (pre-arranged pattern). But, as a basic movement, we open our hands into the shape of Hakko without being conscious of the action itself."

Then what can you do with this hand after abandoning all force? It is shown in the photos on the page 64 and 65. In fact, you can perform quite amazing actions with that hand.

Hakko Nage (eighth light throw) is also the famous representative technique of Hakkoryu. You might not have such doubts if you could watch this technique with your own eyes, but when you view this technique only through photos, you probably doubt why the opponent does not simply release his grasping hands. If he did so, he could easily escape from the throw. But actually he cannot do this.

One can make his hand a "non-resisting hand" by opening it in the Hakko shape, which you do not stretch out nor hold by force. Because of the relationship between one and the opponent, the opponent

Hakko Nage photos 5-3
(Eighth-light Throw, Kaiden level)

The technique of Hakko Nage from the Kaiden level is done as follows: When one is grasped by both wrists, at first he opens his hands in the Hakko shape and then throws the opponent by crossing his arms to unbalance and control him. This Hakko Nage is performed instantaneously,

Chapter 5
Open my hand in the Hakko shape

and accordingly, you do not find anything extraordinary. But if you watch it in a continuous photo sequence, you are surely skeptical and wonder "Why does the opponent not just release his grasping hands, then he can very easily escape from the throw?" The answer to that question is the secret of this technique, and is concealed in the way one opens his grasped hands in the Hakko shape. Namely, he uses "non-resisting hands" and therefore, the opponent perceives no uncomfortable or threatening feeling in his grasping hands. Then he is simply guided by his grasping wrists/arms, while he keeps that natural feeling, and has no chance to release his grip. In many normal circumstances, when one tries to move another using power, a power clash happens. In this case, one can notice a chance or moment to react and possibly resist or release one's hand to escape from grasping. In this technique, there is no such chance.

feels no resistance, so he feels his hands are naturally connected with one's arms/wrists. And, because of that feeling he just keeps grasping one's wrists, even though his body is moved via those connections. You can hardly believe what is happening in front of you. You need to experience it yourself to get that strange feeling, which might be explained as you having no chance or ability to release your gripping hands. If the thrower puts force into his arms/hands, then it might become a totally different situation.

For the people who do not understand what is happening, it might look like a performance and not a real technique. Well, the secret of this strange motion has already been explained above.

◉ What you can do by Kaishu (open hands)

Okuyama 2nd Soke says, "You can make closer contact with the opponent with an open hand than with a closed hand, which is also an important key factor in controlling the other."

The end stage of Shuto Jime (Sword-Hand Lock, 2nd Dan level) is shown in [photo 5-4]. Here, if the opponent could release his hand he could escape from this tightening, but he actually cannot do it because of the fact explained previously. He cannot find a chance to do so".

Shuto Jime (Sword-Hand Lock, 2nd Dan level)
If one tries this technique with a closed hand (fist), it becomes quite difficult to perform this technique effectively.

photo 5-4

Chapter 5
Open my hand in the Hakko shape

Here, it is important that you secure close contact with the opponent using an open hand. If one tries this technique with his hand closed, and attempts to move it down, he will never succeed. Okuyama 2nd Soke showed me that example. Again I found it marvellous. I now sense that there is a deeper meaning to opening one's hand in the Hakko shape than simply having an open or closed hand. It is not the case of whether to put force in your hand or not. Of course, the shape of the hand is different, but the important point is something else, like the nature of the difference of whether to open the hand in the Hakko shape or just open it.

Now the other technique, Ushiro Hakko Dori (Rear Eighth-Light Art, 4th Dan level) is shown in [photos 5-5]. In this chapter, we introduce a lot of the Hakko shape hands in techniques.

The opponent grasps both of Okuyama 2nd Soke's wrists from behind and Okuyama 2nd Soke opens his grasped hands in the Hakko shape. Then Okuyama 2nd Soke reverses his position with the opponent, from front to back, which looks a miraculous feat. The action shown in [photos 5-5], no.1-5, where Okuyama 2nd Soke brings both his hands to the front, was already introduced in Chapter 3, in the technique of Tachi Gyaku Go Katame (Standing Reverse Five Hold, a Kaiden level technique), so I will skip its explanation here. However, here I will say again that it is a really surprising action.

Furthermore, the biggest surprise is the last controlling method which I could not believe at all.

Okuyama 2nd Soke controls the opponent (both of whom are standing) by clamping the wrist, elbow and shoulder of the opponent using his own right arm. Okuyama 2nd Soke insists his left arm, which clenches the opponent, should be done with an open hand. That arm looks as if it is a ridged bar and nothing else, so it should not matter if it has an open or closed hand. But Okuyama 2nd Soke maintains that it should definitely be an open hand.

"The palm should push the opponent's body backwards, otherwise one cannot control the opponent. If it is with a closed hand (fist) you cannot push the opponent's body backwards."

The above motion to rotate the arm in a counter clockwise fashion with an open hand is combined with a raising arm motion to lift the opponent's body up and he loses his balance.

In fact, with a closed hand, it is not easy to realize this subtle movement. Regardless, if you push the opponent with your arm in the same way as above (let the palm face the side of the opponent's body), but while holding your hand in a closed fist, you feel that this posture is quite awkward, i.e., something is wrong.

I suppose such differences are caused by the condition and relationship between the wrist – ulna – radius, muscle of forearm, and subsequently, affects the mobility of the elbow and upper arm as a result. You can cut into the other's body using Shuto (hand sword) but not using your fist. It is not only a mental image, but the strike itself is actually meant to cut into the opponent's body as if using a Katana.

"To listen to Hakko" works very well for a great variety of situations and therefore, you should keep it in your mind that you should listen to Hakko for any changing circumstances, although it might be difficult to do so.

You should not get stiff or stray from the path you must take during a life or death crisis. This is an enormous undertaking to manage mentally, or consciously. Therefore, you do not need to worry, and just make an open hand. That's it. Then you will definitely abandon making a fist.

"That is wonderful. It never brings about a good result when one uses their fist and puts force in it. A fist can be used only to hit another person. Hitting each other can never make people happy."

Now I remember one of the three main principles of Hakkoryu is "no injury".

Ushiro Hakko Dori
(Rear Eighth-Light Art, 4th Dan level)

photos 5-5

Chapter 5
Open my hand in the Hakko shape

This is a marvellous technique. Okuyama 2nd Soke, who has been grasped by both of his wrists from behind, guides each of the opponent's grasping hands to his front quite smoothly and naturally. This is due to the effect of his open hands (Hakko) which have an excellent positioning feature when open in Hakko. It becomes quite hard when one tries the same action with their hands grasped while holding a fist with each. It is especially important that one uses an open hand with his left arm when using it a ridged bar to put into the opponent's right armpit.

In the last stage of Ushiro Hakko Dori, one needs to move his arm deep up in the opponent's armpit. Without this motion one cannot control the opponent. Once you attempt to do the same motion using a closed hand (fist), you cannot control the opponent effectively. The freedom of the arm with an open hand appears small but actually it is big and that large degree of freedom produces this different effect.

Chapter 6

The secret of "pain"

◈ Touch, press, release; these three steps make the technique work

Hakkoryu is represented by its image of having "painful techniques". But if you observe the result of these techniques, the techniques do not seem that painful at all. But even those techniques which start in a common way actually give the opponent an enormous degree of pain, but this might be caused by some form of mental effect.

Gakun (the action of the Gakun grip), the technique which begins at the 3rd Dan level is the personification of the painful techniques of Hakkoryu. By this technique, one just touches the other's wrist gently and, "That's it". The opponent should feel that only light force is applied to his wrist but he receives enormous pain as a result. And that is why it is so strange.

"In Hakkoryu we do not apply techniques using force and it is the same for Gakun. You should never grasp the opponent's wrist strongly or tightly." Okuyama 2nd Soke explains this while putting his hand on the opponent's lower arm, then sliding it down the opponent's forearm with a light grip. He is just touching the forearm with a light grip so it can slide down smoothly. At the end of this sliding motion his gripping hand stops right over the opponent's wrist.

"You apply Gakun at the place where your grip clicks-in and stops naturally. You never grasp it strongly or tightly but just as if hooking your hand on the wrist."

When Okuyama 2nd Soke changes his grip's angle against the wrist, the opponent receives sharp pain and falls down to the floor. You can expect the technique is coming and prepare it, but it is still very painful. Although one

Chapter 6
The secret of "pain"

How to apply Gakun.
You should never bend your hand/wrist using force but just slide your hand from top to bottom and stop your grip at the end of this sliding movement. Generally speaking, it is just hanging on, but not grasping. In the flying trapeze of the circus, the performers hold ropes in the same way. It is so strange. You cannot always grasp something strongly if you put force in your hands.

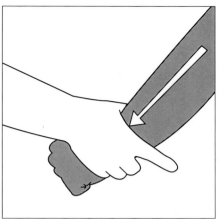

illustration 6-1

never presses the point hard, it is still extremely painful. The point must be a very sensitive weak spot, right? We tend to think this, but it is not the case at all.

It is the place just above the protrusion of the bone located on the outside of wrist. Please try to push that point yourself. You probably do not feel much pain.

"Gakun needs the precondition that the opponent puts force or tension into the point to resist the action being applied to him. By putting force or tension there, that place turns into a weak point. And it is also an important precondition that one should not apply force within his own hand to bend the opponent's wrist."

Such technical aspects should be common for all Hakkoryu techniques, as a "relaxed person always wins over a tense one"

"You use the lower inside portion of your index finger, near its base where the knuckle is, to touch the opponent's wrist. And you never just press on the wrist. At the moment you touch the opponent's wrist with the lower inside of your index finger, you push there in the manner of applying Shiatsu."

There is no need to explain here about the unique Koho Shiatsu of Hakkoryu. It is, of course, used to cure illness but it can also work as a painful technique. And how awfully painful it is!

Gakun (3rd Dan level)   photos 6-1

Okuyama 2nd Soke just holds the opponent's wrist lightly. But such light holding can create enormous pain. That is Gakun. Okuyama 2nd Soke seems like he is doing nothing in the photos but you can guess what is happening at that moment by watching the face of his opponent, Mr. Okawa, shown in the 3rd photo.

Chapter 6
The secret of "pain"

"You also should not apply Shiatsu by force. You should use abdominal pressure but not the force of your arm. After hearing this, most people tend to put force in their abdomen, which is also not correct. We teach our students that the "Abdomen contains the negative aspect of power, while the back has the positive one." That is why, for Koho Shiatsu, people have to learn Seisoku no Ho (the way of correct breathing) to avoid putting force only in the abdomen."

Here, let's explain Seisoku no Ho briefly.
1st Gently inhale by expanding the rib cage and pulling in the abdomen
2nd Then gently exhale by expanding the abdomen
3rd Exhale further
Here, the breathing operates in three processes:
1st stage: Your force is naturally settled into your hips
2nd stage: Your force is naturally settled into your abdomen
3rd stage: You can create the same level of tension in both the hips and abdomen.

The most important point for this type of breathing is that force is

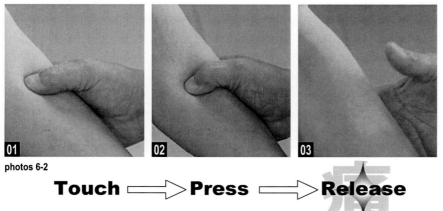

The three processes of Koho Shiatsu are shown in the 3 photos above. First you touch a place with the thumb and press there. Then you release your thumb, and in that last step, when you release your thumb, a trigger to stimulate pain in the nerves occurs. It is quite strange that pain occurs at the moment of release but not when it is pressed. From the perspective of Bujutsu, this process has merit in learning to avoid a situation where one sticks too much to the target.

photos 6-2

Touch ⟹ Press ⟹ Release

naturally settled into both the hips and abdomen. Anyhow, we will explain more about this breathing method later.

"We perform Shiatsu itself in three steps, meaning, we first touch the place being treated, then we press there, and finally, release the pressure. At the instant you release pressure, the person feels some pain."

This is the sophisticated way in which the curing force reaches the target point located deep in a body. If one presses the point only using force it might damage the system.

There is deep meaning in the fact that one feels pain only at the instant the applier releases his finger pressure. Because the pain occurs only for an instant, this is the reason why it works well.

As a technique of Bujutsu, pain itself cannot be the sole purpose, but a means to lead the opponent to take some action. In that sense the approach you take to apply pain should be deep enough, and done in an instant.

If you can prepare for the anticipated pain, you can probably avoid making any unnecessary reaction to some extent. But then the opponent will likely increase their power to cause you more pain. As a result it becomes a "cat and mouse game". On the contrary, if you have Gakun applied to you, at that moment your brain stops conscious thinking. First your body reacts against the pain automatically. Then, when you recover conscious thought, you have already fallen down to the floor. But what a strange feeling it is that you do not have any unpleasant feeling.

Okuyama 2nd Soke says, "Our techniques apply the same concept as Shiatsu. And that is also why it can be good for health."

It is really a phenomenal and a sophisticated action that can be done in an instant.

◉ What pain causes

In Hakkoryu they say if you try to apply a technique, it does not work. It sounds like a very philosophical way of thinking, but their main theme is how to become free from tension when you try to apply techniques. And, conversely, they also teach how you can be free from mental disturbance, which makes you tense and stiff when a technique is applied on you.

But of course this is very difficult. When you become fixated on not

Chapter 6
The secret of "pain"

having a technique applied to you, you can never totally avoid tension or straining of some kind. Especially at the moment when the opponent is actually applying a technique on you, it is extremely difficult to relax without being conscious of, and reacting to the technique. I now guess the key to solve this question might be "how to handle pain".

"By all means, you need gentleness in Hakkoryu. But actually, this is difficult because not all people around you are gentle-minded people. For people who are not so gentle, you just apply a technique on them. By receiving pain, they start learning how to deal with pain and will grow gentle-minded during the course of Hakkoryu training. We expect this effect for everybody."

It must be true that the more you strain yourself, the more pain you receive. At the beginning one cannot help becoming conscious of it and straining themselves, which causes even more pain as a consequence. There is only one way to escape from that situation, just relax and avoid straining. It sounds like a dilemma but the solution is very clear.

"In the past we often practised in a rather hard way. Accordingly, after training it often happened that we felt so much pain all over our body that we could not even raise light chopsticks during meals. But in such situations one cannot put force in their muscles so you are free from tension. In that sense, such training could not have been so bad."

That sounds like the ultimate goal during those times was very hard training indeed. Anyway, one needs pain to develop as a human being, so I understood the point. When we think over the meaning of "pain", we associate words with it, such as "destruction" and "damage" and therefore, it creates fear in our mind. But if the pain happens for a brief moment, it is just a form of stimulation. Then we do not have to fear it. In fact, in Koho Shiatsu, the most basic concept is to activate human physiology by stimulation, which causes a pain reaction in the body.

Considering this from the point of this book's theme of mental effect, pain can cause fear and caution, which creates straining and tension in one's body or narrowing of one's mind. But in pain itself you can find the solution to how you can become free from it. Hmm...... This has deep meaning. I feel as if I was receiving a lecture about how to live my life.

Ude Osae Dori photos 6-3
(Arm Pin Art, 2nd Dan level)

As a reply to my request to demonstrate an extremely painful technique, Okuyama 2nd Soke showed me this one. First, Okuyama 2nd Soke turns the opponent's grasping hand so that his small finger side comes up, then Okuyama 2nd Soke cuts down with his right arm using Shuto. This motion causes the opponent enormous pain. This technique is so dangerous that Okuyama 2nd Soke can easily break the opponent's wrist or elbow bones, but that is not the aim of this technique. So, Okuyama 2nd Soke changes the direction of his Shuto to allow for a throw and lets the opponent turn his body and fall down on the floor.

Chapter 6
The secret of "pain"

Mune Osae Dori photos 6-4
(Chest Pin Art, 2nd Dan level)

As a reply to my further request for a more painful technique, Okuyama 2nd Soke showed the following. The fact that my request made the opponent, Mr. Okawa, very unhappy, clearly showed in his facial expression.

I could see Okuyama 2nd Soke's motion to turn the opponent's grasping hand with the small finger side up. The intent to apply this technique does not show up in the movement however, which is the strong point of Hakkoryu. And subsequently, it causes tremendous pain.

This photo shows the situation 3 seconds after the ending posture. Mr. Okawa could not stand up for a while. Maybe he felt so good after receiving such enormous pain that he was enjoying a little relaxation himself.

Chapter 7

About Kamae (Posturing)

◉ The secret of left foot forward posturing

The Japanese word Kamae (posturing, or positioning) also has the meaning of the way in which people use intention or will in their daily life. In Bujutsu and other fighting arts there exist different shapes of posturing based on their unique features. The difference in these postures demonstrates the different cases against which they are preparing. For boxing, they put their fists in front of the face and this is quite natural considering the risk, based on their fighting rules.

Okuyama 2nd Soke says, "But if you try to prepare yourself according to the way in which you expect the opponent to attack you, it might restrict your mind. Such a way of thinking might have a negative effect in Bujutsu. One should be able to react against any manner of attack in Bujutsu." In fact, if the opponent pierces your abdomen using a knife while you guard your face, that is the end.

Actually, posturing in Hakkoryu places its importance on your future actions, not what you guard against.

By the way, Hakkoryu has Kenjutsu (sword) techniques as well. Because of its popular image as self-defence Jujutsu, this may seem surprising, but it gives you a clearer view of understanding the concept of posture, or Kamae, when you watch their Ken-versus-Ken (sword-versus-sword) posturing. Let's start with the posture for a Ken-versus-Ken situation.

In modern Kendo, and even old styles of Kenjutsu, they set up their posture based on a Ken-versus-Ken match, and accordingly, they have several common postures. This is because when attacking with a sword, there are certain patterns of attack that are also common and might happen in most

Chapter 7
About Kamae (Posturing)

Posturing of Hakkoryu Kenjutsu

The basic posturing in Hakkoryu Kenjtsu is a left foot forward stance, which is rarely observed in modern Kendo and each respective ryuha of old school Kenjutsu. If you try this posturing, the first time you feel a little strange, but your body faces to the front naturally with this stance.

photos 7-1

cases. In Hakkoryu, their posturing looks similar to the common sword stances of other styles, but there is one point that is totally different from all other Kenjutsu schools. It is quite surprising that they assume their Kamae with the left foot forward (refer to [photos 7-1]).

In Japanese Kenjutsu, it is not allowed to take a southpaw stance, which is allowed for the most of fighting arts and sports. Maybe this does not have a very important meaning and is just a variation of left or right stance. So, this southpaw posturing of Hakkoryu may appear to be a trick, so to speak. But then what is its merit?

If you try this southpaw posture, your body automatically faces to the front (i.e., you do not make a half-open stance, or Hanmi).

In Hakkoryu, the basic posture is Seitai (front-facing stance) and not a half-open stance. So for Hakkoryu, body mechanics (i.e., posturing) are the same for both Jujutsu and Kenjutsu. A half-open stance has more benefit for defence because you can minimize the area which is visible to the opponent, and thus, vulnerable to attack. But considering this front-facing stance, which is considered highly irregular in traditional Kenjutsu, Hakkoryu has no philosophy to minimize the risk for defensive purposes, based on a statistical theory that takes into account various possible ways of attacking.

This point is exactly what I expected.

Saying "It should be like this." Okuyama 2nd Soke assumed a left foot forward stance while taking up a Bokuto (wooden sword). Against the left foot forward stance that Okuyama 2nd Soke assumed, the opponent, Mr. Okawa, assumed the normal right foot forward stance. Their distance is far enough that Mr. Okawa's Bokuto cannot reach Okuyama 2nd Soke, even if he takes a normal forward step.

But even at such a great distance, Okuyama 2nd Soke just took one normal step forward and his Bokuto could reach Mr. Okawa. The length of Okuyama 2nd Soke's step, or stride, should actually be less than Mr. Okawa's because he is shorter than Mr. Okawa.

"You should use Ayumi Ashi (walking step) instead of Tsugi Ashi (shuffle step) as a fundamental step. You should start with the rear foot as you would walk, that offers you an advantage."

Hmmm, if you start your step with the back foot then you can move your body further forward. Conversely, if you start your step with the front foot, your motion becomes quicker, but you cannot gain the advantage of a longer forward displacement, although at first it looks like this is possible. It looks like as though you try to make yourself taller by standing up on the toes.

Then, I thought I could perform the same thing, but in a right foot forward stance instead. So, I tried to start my step with the left foot (rear foot), which I though was logical but I could not advance forward as smoothly as I could in the left foot forward stance. Besides, if I start assuming the left foot forward stance instead of the right foot forward stance, both the right arm and left foot are forward which makes it difficult to extend the tip of the Bokuto toward the opponent.

"Of course, in a real situation there are more complicated matters at work,

Chapter 7
About Kamae (Posturing)

The secret of left foot front posturing in which you can always win with Tsuki (thrusting) in competition

photos 7-2

You keep the distance so that a forward step with the right foot in a normal right front stance cannot reach the opponent. But Okuyama 2nd Soke, with his left front posturing, steps forward with his right foot and can reach the opponent easily. The photo 04 shows the end stage where his right arm and foot are both in front. As long as you grip the Bokuto with the right hand forward, the stance with the right foot forward has the longest reachable distance, and this is common for both a right or left front posture. But the difference in the process or mechanics of stepping causes the difference in reach. To describe it more plainly, to start your step using the rear foot creates the advantage. But there are other elements, such as the way the hand grips which might be combined with this way of stepping to create the advantage. In an actual situation the elements in judging combative distance (Maai) varies in a much more complicated way.

81

based on the theory of motion, and in a real fight things might not happen in such a simple way. But at least I can say the posturing should include the next motion in its shape. It should not just be a preparation for the assumed method in which the opponent will attack.

◈ The secret of Hakko Kamae

Now we perform empty hand posturing.

"You should assume a natural posture so that you can react against any kind of attack. As such, we do not have various postures or stances that prepare us to guard against certain types of attack."

Although Okuyama 2nd Soke says this, there exists one posture in Hakkoryu called Hakko Kamae, as shown in [photos 7-3]. Even though Okuyama 2nd Soke said they did not have such postures, I still thought they

Hakko Kamae (posturing)

Position your right arm so that it is stretched forward to cover your face. Put your left arm behind your body so that your opponent cannot see it from the front.

photos 7-3

Chapter 7
About Kamae (Posturing)

You can block or deflect the opponent's straight punch by just putting your right outstretched arm straight forward. You would never notice its effect if you did not know this defence. It is a surprising and unexpectedly wonderful way of defence.

photos 7-4

did. But he was not being untruthful or misleading.

"Hakko posturing is not a stance in which you wait for the attack, it is the posture that is assumed when one is attacked."

Then the posturing should vary according to the type of attack, or so I thought. But if I watch this posturing very carefully, it assumes a stance which is applicable against any kind of attack. In that sense it can be a natural posture.

Okuyama 2nd Soke just put his right arm straight forward which guards his Seichu Sen (body center line). At least with this outstretched arm he can guard his face against the opponent's straight or hook punch.

Speaking in the extreme, if you can take this posture even in a sudden attack situation, you can minimize your level of damage. This way of posturing has such an effect. This must be the very unique posture of Hakkoryu, which specializes in self-defence.

I understood more clearly after watching its actual usage. The outstretched

Yokomen Uchi Dori
(Arm Pin Art, 4th Dan level)

One can avoid the attacker's side hook punch by putting your right hand and arm straight forward. Then, capture the attacker's left wrist in the Gakun to throw him down, and control him using an arm pin. All the movements shown in photos 1 to 6 occur in one rapid movement.

photos 7-5

arm can block the opponent's straight punch aimed at one's face. That is true. But I never thought you could defend yourself against a hook punch using the same outstretched arm. And it really works.

Besides, because you keep your arm stretched forward, you can leverage it immediately for your counter technique. You can see how quickly Okuyama 2nd Soke executed his counter attack by applying Gakun to the opponent, as seen in the technique Yokomen Uchi Dori (Side of Head Strike Art, 4th Dan level) shown in [photos 7-5].

As a matter of fact, Hakkoryu, which is based on the concept of self-defense, has no attacking techniques. This means, as long as one is not attacked, nothing can happen. That is why it was surprising that the Kamae, or posturing of

Chapter 7
About Kamae (Posturing)

Hakkoryu is so active. This is because I thought that ultimately, assuming a posture was a defensive action to passively wait for the opponent's attack. But in Hakkoryu they do not believe in posturing in such a passive way.

"You can never anticipate what attack shall come. So it is no use to anticipate it. It is much more important to think over what reaction you should take, or to prepare yourself for how well you can move in reaction."

Well, it is no use to worry about attacks beforehand. You could spend all of your life thinking over how to prepare against thousands of different attacks. But the teachings of Hakkoryu are not so haphazard. The posture itself is equipped with a fine-tuning effect so that you can instantly take the best action of defense against a sudden attack in a very sophisticated way.

You do not need to worry about what may happen tomorrow. You only need to prepare your mind so that you can survive in any crisis. If we can live in such a mindset, it would be wonderful.

Chapter 8

The importance of "fingers" and their strongest direction

◉ The reason why Okuyama 2nd Soke cannot be pushed back

Here, Okuyama 2nd Soke blocks the opponent's Seiken Tsuki (straight fist punch) with his palm as shown in [photo 8-1].

Okuyama 2nd Soke says, "If you do this normally, your hand will be pushed back by his fist."

Considering the difference of weight between the two, I do not think Okuyama 2nd Soke can hold the opponent's punch using only one hand/arm. So I think he's correct.

Then Okuyama 2nd Soke made one small change.

photo 8-1

"Now he [Okawa Shihan] cannot push me forward."

It was indeed true, Okawa Shihan could no longer push Okuyama 2nd Soke forward. On the contrary, he is pushed back by Okuyama 2nd Soke's single-hand block. (Please refer to [photos 8-2].)

Then I tried it myself. It is strange that I cannot put force into my fist that is pushing. What happened? I guess it was the same "trick" Okuyama 2nd Soke performed on Okawa Shihan.

Chapter 8
The importance of "fingers" and their strongest direction

The positioning looks the same as is shown on [photo 8-1], but when Okawa Shihan tried to push Okuyama 2nd Soke's hand he could not put force into his fist. On the contrary, Okuyama 2nd Soke pushed him back without using much force.

photos 8-2

"I shifted my blocking hand a little bit to the small finger side. In fact, a hand has a certain direction where force works most effectively. Placing the middle finger as the center line, the small finger side can pull better and thumb side can push better. As a result, if you hold the opponent's punch between the middle finger and thumb, he can push you forward easily because it is the place where the opponent's hand can push most efficiently. In Karate or boxing they try to punch with the knuckles around the index and middle fingers. This is the reason why they do this. That is also why I hold the opponent's fist with the small finger side where it has direction to pull, and accordingly, it is weak or susceptible to being pushed."

I had no idea of the importance in placing the hands and fingers in their preferred natural directions or positions.

The hand has a natural position with the middle finger as the neutral line, where the thumb side is good at pushing, and the small finger side is good at pulling.

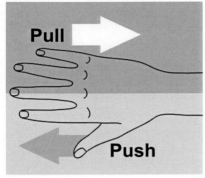

illustration 8-1

Tsuki Mi Dori photos 8-3
(Body Thrust Art, 3rd Dan level)

Okuyama 2nd Soke catches the opponent's straight punch with two hands as if covering it. If you receive the opponent's punch and block hard, your hand may be seriously injured. So you need a sophisticated catch that shifts their thrusting power to the small finger side. As soon as Okuyama 2nd Soke catches the opponent's fist, he immediately applies Gakun to the opponent's wrist and executes the final control. Using only one hand, Okuyama 2nd Soke completely controls the opponent and he cannot move.

On [photos 8-3], the 3rd Dan technique, Tsukimi Dori (Body Thrust Art) is shown, which I had seen before. At that time I could not believe it was possible to be able to block the opponent's punch using only one hand. But after being taught the importance of the mechanics of the human body, I now see this technique differently. A small hidden trick is applied for this technique.

"People tend to regard the mechanics, or physiology of the human body to be as simple as a machine, but it is actually a little bit more delicate and complex."

Okuyama 2nd Soke is correct. As far as I understand, people use the triceps muscle to stretch out the arm, so someone who has strong triceps can push stronger than someone with less developed triceps. My knowledge about human physiology is pretty basic and I regard it as functioning like a machine.

"If you regard human physiology as functioning like a machine, you can never compete with others who have physically stronger muscles than you. But there is no need to give up when a larger person punches you using his increased power."

You still can block such a strong punch using certain tricks of human physiology. Of course such subtle actions are not that easy to perform.

Chapter 8
The importance of "fingers" and their strongest direction

Anyway, you can deal with a human being's strong punch because it is not a gun, meaning, it is still based on human physiology. If you can think in this way, it will affect your mental state quite positively.

◈ The direction to move

You can also apply this method of orientation to your movement.

For example, if your wrist is grasped, which is often seen in Jujutsu techniques, it is not as easy to deal with this situation as it may appear. You cannot pull the opponent's grasping hand easily unless you can use stronger force in your own arm.

"You should pull your grasped hand in the direction of the small finger side. Because a hand is designed to pull from the small finger side, this is quite easy to understand."

On [photos 8-5], Tekagami (Hand Mirror, from the 1st Dan level techniques) is shown. If you watch the sequence carefully you might notice that Okuyama 2nd Soke raises his grasped right hand from the small finger side. The mechanics of the human body are complex and there is a large degree

Tekagami photos 8-5
(Hand Mirror, 1st Dan level)

Okuyama 2nd Soke, who is grasped by both wrists from the front, raises his right hand by pulling inside, leading with the small finger, then up, and he executes a lock to the opponent's wrist. Okuyama 2nd Soke then changes the side of his hand he is using from the little finger side to the thumb side (i.e., using the base of the thumb and index finger), and quickly drops the wrist down.

In this case, Okuyama 2nd Soke has both wrists grasped by two attackers, one on each side. Then, he pulls both attackers to his front quite easily. This is accomplished by moving both of his hands with the small finger side leading.

photo 8-4

Chapter 8
The importance of "fingers" and their strongest direction

of freedom in its movement, so it is quite possible that one may try to pull their hand from the thumb side—and actually it might happen this way more often than it does by the small finger side. We probably could not easily detect which is the correct motion and which is not. But if such methods are left vague, and we attempt to find the correct motion that makes sense in Bujutsu techniques, it might take hundreds years.

In Hakkoryu, they teach how to find the most reasonable method through technique. Beginners especially tend to focus on the phenomenal or miraculous aspects of martial arts rather than technique and subsequently, they have to spend a lot of time in vain and cannot discover the most important matters. We hear about such stories quite often in the Bujutsu community. I think this the secret of Hakkoryu, and why their students can master the art so quickly and skillfully. Because of this, I think everybody can master it.

"If we focus on the fingers, the small finger side naturally closes and the thumb side opens or releases. You should leverage those natural mechanics in daily life. For instance, when you hold the handle of a bag, you should not hold it tightly with the thumb and index finger because gripping is a job performed best using the small finger and ring finger. Further, if you maintain a grip with the small finger, ring finger and middle finger that is not too tight, you can hold your bag much stronger and surely. If you apply such logical actions in daily life, you will master the mechanics of Bujutsu automatically."

I now remember something. I was often invited to their dinner parties and I noticed one thing. Every time they made a toast, all of them held their glasses with their index finger off and kept it straight. So they held their glasses using the small finger side, without the index finger. Hmmm, they really do practice this method in daily life.

Chapter 8
The importance of "fingers" and their strongest direction

The theory of finger direction can be applied to holding the handle of a bag. If you do not hold the handle using the thumb side of the hand tightly, but rather, by using the last three fingers, or the small finger, ring finger and middle finger as if just hanging lightly onto it, you can hold the bag stronger, and can avoid it being suddenly snatched away. **photos 8-6**

Chapter 9

Danger arises suddenly without time to prepare

◈ Do not stick to prejudice or get lost

First, please look at the following photo, then form a mental image of the 2nd photo, which shows the result of this 1st one, [photos 9-1]. Next, please look at [photos 9-1], no.2. Is that the same as you imagined? Especially if you are an experienced martial artist, you should feel something is out of place, shouldn't you?

The mismatch comes from the preconception that you thought the attacker, shown in the 1st photo, held the knife in his right hand but in actuality, it was held in his left hand.

photos 9-1

Chapter 9
Danger arises suddenly without time to prepare

If you have such preconceived notions as, "In most cases, the attacker should not be left-handed. In most Budo training the opponent attacks on their right side. If the attacker holds a Katana with both hands, his right hand should be in front of his left. Or, if the attacker holds it with one hand, he should use his right hand." If this is your prejudice, then you can hardly imagine such a situation as is shown in [photos 9-1], no.2.

In this case, whether the opponent uses their right hand or left hand is quite an important point. If one avoids to the outside of the attacking arm, he is safe because of the arm's freedom of movement caused by the structure of the human body. But if one avoids the attack to the inside of the arm, then the risk continues. So there is a turning point where one is safe or not when choosing to avoid the attack to right or left. It worries me that I might choose the wrong side in such a situation.

"Do not worry. You will never fail." Okuyama 2nd Soke replied while smiling.

But I am still uncertain that one might make the mistake of choosing the wrong side, because, in reality, there is no prearrangement or rehearsal.

By the way, this time the demonstration was done without any rehearsal. So, Okuyama 2nd Soke did not know which side the opponent would attack from. Normally, for such demonstrations we do a rehearsal. But this time, just for fun, we did this without rehearsing. We started this section without setting the theme beforehand, but consequently, "without rehearsal" became the theme of this chapter automatically.

From the very beginning, Hakkoryu has placed importance on self-defense. As such, in self-defense, you should train for unpredictable situations where you never have a chance to judge with which hand the attacker may carry a weapon. Therefore, in Hakkoryu, they surely have some secret way to discern this quickly.

"First, you should not stick to preconceptions. Most people who may be confronted by a person wielding a weapon in his hand appearing in front of them would likely be quite surprised and focus their attention automatically onto the weapon itself. At that point, they have lost sight of the total situation.

If one's attention is drawn to, or restricted to, a very narrow point or area, they have to guess at the other areas that they cannot see. And accordingly, one needs information to glean with which hand the attacker may hold his weapon. On the contrary, if one can see the whole situation, they can imagine what might come next. You do not need such information as whether it is with the right or left in such a context. Although you cannot guess if the attacker may come in with the right or left, you can judge using your senses what you should do in reaction, based on your imagination of the next stage.

"If you fixate on one small point, you tend to restrain yourself. If you can just relax, you can make an appropriate reaction automatically, which is the most important point. If you are not restricted, you can easily react against whatever attacks you may encounter. That can be done without rehearsal."

Well, if you understand the concept that you do not have to worry about the attacker's weapon, you can then be free from restraining yourself, and can see the entirety of the situation. Accordingly, you can naturally sense what comes next. In the beginning of this chapter we discussed whether the knife may come from the right or left, but it probably does not matter at all. This is because you can only see the next stage if you disregard whether or not the attack starts from the right or left.

In Hakkoryu, they also hold public demonstrations, although these are not frequently held. In such demonstrations, they do not normally make up any specific scenario beforehand. All their performances are made without rehearsals.

At the instant the attacker thrusts the knife straight forward, he can move the knife easily to his inside, but not to his outside. Accordingly, it is dangerous to evade to his inside.

photos 9-2

Chapter 9
Danger arises suddenly without time to prepare

"If we set a specific scenario or routine, we cannot help sticking to it. So, the best way is to do a performance without a specific plan or scenario."

And what a splendid motion they show! They execute their movements to the right and left quite freely and naturally.

◈ Still anxious about which side, right or left?

Hakkoryu has a huge variety of techniques and it is quite a task just to remember all of them. Besides, they all have both right and left versions, so the total number doubles. Then, by human nature, we tend to omit some of them. For instance, if the opponent come in with a right attack then we execute this technique, or if he comes in with a left attack, we use these techniques. However, I understand it is prohibited to practice in such a way in Hakkoryu.

"Every technique should be practiced equally, on both the right and left side. If you prefer one side over another, that is "sticking" (i.e., narrowing your focus). So, you should avoid such preferences and keep yourself neutral, not right or left."

In fact, they have right and left versions for all their techniques, including those techniques with quite complex movements. And they perform all these techniques on the right and left side quite excellently. If they have to think every time about using the right hand if grasped by left hand, they could never perform all these techniques as smoothly as they demonstrate. Because they place their attention on the complete situation, they can perform right and left variations smoothly and naturally, without thinking about the right or left at every stage.

Then I discovered a remarkably surprising technique, which I do not fully comprehend. It is called Oikake Dori (Pursuit Art, 4th Dan level, refer to [photos 9-4]). This technique starts from a situation where one is grasped on the back of the head from behind. As soon as the opponent grasps the back of his head, he turns from his upper body and slips his body and head under the opponent's grasping arm from front to back, then he presses up on the opponent's arm to lock it. It depends on which arm the opponent uses that determines if one should turn to the right or left. But, because the opponent attacks from behind, one should not be able to tell which arm the opponent

In a case where the attacker is armed with a weapon, you tend to focus your mind on the weapon itself. The more you focus your attention on it, the narrower your sight becomes. In such a situation, you need to decide from which side, right or left, the opponent will launch his attack. On the contrary, if you can focus your attention on the whole opponent, or situation, you can determine his next action and prepare yourself against his potential attack by knowing what you should do.

Please just watch the action shown in the two photos, [photos 9-3]. Looking at the right photo, you think, "This should be the left hand." But when you view the photo on the left, you might think, "It does not matter if it is the left or right."

photos 9-3

uses to hold the back of his head. Nevertheless, Okuyama 2nd Soke turns and slips his upper body under the opponent's arm straight away, quite smoothly. It is so strange how he is able to do it.

Okuyama 2nd Soke says, "You can turn after touching the opponent's hand with your own hand to check which side hand he is using." But, if I was in this situation, I could not recognize which side hand the opponent used, even after touching his hand.

"Do not worry. Everybody can understand it." Okuyama 2nd Soke said while smiling.

Hearing what Okuyama 2nd Soke says "everybody can understand", I thought he meant that, while not everybody can determine which side, everybody can understand what they should do.

It is quite all right then, and we do not need worry. Even if the opponent's attack comes from behind where we cannot see it, or with which side hand he uses, we can see the whole picture because we do not get stuck on the point of which side hand he uses. Our entire body turns as a sensor, so we can feel the opponent's action not only with our eyes. Okuyama 2nd Soke probably senses what action he should take at the very instant the opponent grasps the back of his head. It can obviously be seen that Okuyama 2nd Soke never used the wrong side hand to capture the opponent's grasping hand even once in all the attempts.

◈ Calmness of mind

It should be the goal that one can react to any sudden crisis situation, as a result of accumulated practice of Goshinjutsu (self-defense arts) and Bujutsu. And no doubt, Hakkoryu has that goal, too. We should realize this from the words of Okuyama 2nd Soke: "No problem. It's OK."

I suppose if one has a calm mind, their sensitivity as human beings can be improved. It is the opposite situation for people who get stuck on one thing, they feel fear and uneasiness. When one feels continuously uneasy, their sensitivity drops drastically, as you may well know. However, if you can say to yourself "No problem. It's OK", you can react to the situation in the best way.

Previously, I mentioned the theme of "Let's do it without rehearsal." When I asked Okuyama 2nd Soke to do his demonstration in this way, he replied to me while smiling, "No problem. It's OK." In fact, Okuyama 2nd Soke always replies to me with "No problem. It's OK." With such calmness of mind, Okuyama 2nd Soke can reply this way every time, which most of us cannot. Of course, Okuyama 2nd Soke can say this with a background where he has actually dealt with so many such situations. But let's leave it there. It might not even matter if we do not have such deep and widespread experience. If we can simply say in any situation, "No problem. It's OK.", then our sensitivity is surely improved, which increases our ability to react spontaneously.

In fact, the reality is that most things happen in this world without warning or expectation. Very few things turn out as anticipated. And that is why I wanted to try to perform a technique without rehearsal, just once.

I felt a little scared, but that no problem, was it?

Oikake Dori photos 9-4
(4th Dan level)

This technique, Oikake Dori, starts with the situation that the opponent has chased you down and grabbed the back of your head from the rear. While the opponent holds the back of his head, he turns his upper body to slip his body and head under the opponent's

Chapter 9
Danger arises suddenly without time to prepare

grasping arm from front to back, then applies Kime (a control) to the opponent's wrist using Gakun and forces him down to the floor. He turns his body either clockwise, or counter-clockwise, according to which hand (right or left) the opponent uses to attack from behind.

Chapter 10

One can only concentrate for a short time

◈ Training should be done within 20 minutes

When you enter a Hakkoryu Dojo (training hall) you will always see the following notice, [photo 10-1]. It says, "The training time in Hakkoryu should be within 20 minutes." When it is hot in the summer nobody wants to continue training for many hours while sweating. Such a thing never happens in Hakkoryu.

Okuyama 2nd Soke says, "In the first place, it is important to train with concentration and one cannot continue their concentration for longer than 20

The notice that is placed on the wall of the H.Q. Dojo, declaring, "One training session should be done within 20 minutes."

photo 10-1

minutes. That is why we set our training time so short, and because of this reduced training time, everyone can train with a concentrated mind."

Recently, I conducted an interview with a craftsman who works in a risky environment. At that time, he told me that he can only seriously concentrate 15-20 minutes a day, so he tries to schedule the most important task during that short period.

Without knowing this important point (i.e., one thinks they can fully concentrate all day), one tends to continue long hours of training without a concentrated mind. As a result he/she cannot attain any significant achievement. I have had such an experience myself.

As a matter of fact, under such a precondition everybody tries to concentrate on their training for the limited 20 minutes. This time passes very quickly if one's mind is not concentrated. If one watches two hours of TV programing with an absent mind, it ends very fast.

Well then, how is actual training conducted?

◉ The secret of highly integrated training

To observe how the training is done in such a short time as 20 minutes, I asked Okuyama 2nd Soke to show each of the first three techniques from 1st Dan to the 3rd Dan level. I specially did not ask Okuyama 2nd Soke to just show the normal training regimen.

"If you give me 20 minutes, I can even show you all the techniques." Although Okuyama 2nd Soke said this, I thought it must be impossible. Hakkoryu has a huge curriculum, which follows the general pattern of seated techniques first, then half-standing, and finally, standing techniques. And these sets of techniques are further divided by hierarchy in the curriculum within the levels of 1st Dan, 2nd Dan, 3rd Dan, 4th Dan, and so on. So, the number of total techniques is quite substantial!

Then, I made my choice to see the first three techniques from the 1st and 2nd Dan level, as well as the first two from the 3rd Dan level, for a total of eight techniques. All techniques are performed on both the left and right side, which doubles the total number of techniques to sixteen. In addition, the Uke (attacker) and Tori (defender) change roles, so there are a grand total of 36 techniques that will be performed (refer to [photos 10-2]).

photos 10-2

Hakko Dori (1st Dan level)

Simply raise the arm that is grasped by the opponent. You can never raise it up if you use power to compete with the opponent's power. Technical know-how instructs that you need to raise your hand and arm as if to scratch your itchy ear.

Tekagami (1st Dan level)

After mastering how to raise your arm in Hakko Dori, you can easily control your opponent as shown in photo No. 2. Then you drop the opponent down by holding his wrists.

Aiki Nage (Harmonious Spirit Throw, 1st Dan level)

By using the methodology of Tekagami, you start dropping both of your grasped hands. Then you throw the opponent by rotating your left arm with the tip of the thumb on your right hand acting as the center of the circle.

Chapter 10
One can only concentrate for a short time

Matsuba Dori (Pin Needle Art, 2nd Dan level)

The opponent grasps your left wrist with his right hand. You hook your left wrist over his right wrist and control him. You have to leverage the action of raising the left arm without putting force into it, which you learned at the 1st Dan level.

Tekagami (2nd Dan level)

In this level you add Kime (final control or lock) at the end. It should be easily performed if you have mastered the same technique at the 1st Dan level.

  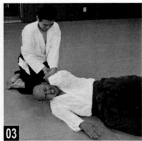

Ude Osae Dori (Arm Pin Art, 2nd Dan level)

When the opponent grasps your upper arm, you apply the same motion as Matsuba Dori to drop the opponent down. It is important to choose the exact place where your arm secures and presses down on the opponent's arm.

Chapter 10
One can only concentrate for a short time

01

02

03

01

02

03

01

02

03

Ude Osae Dori Mochi Mawari (Arm Pin Arrest Lead Around, 3rd Dan level)

Add the following action to the end of the previous Ude Osae Dori to allow the opponent to rise up by controlling his wrist and then to pin him.

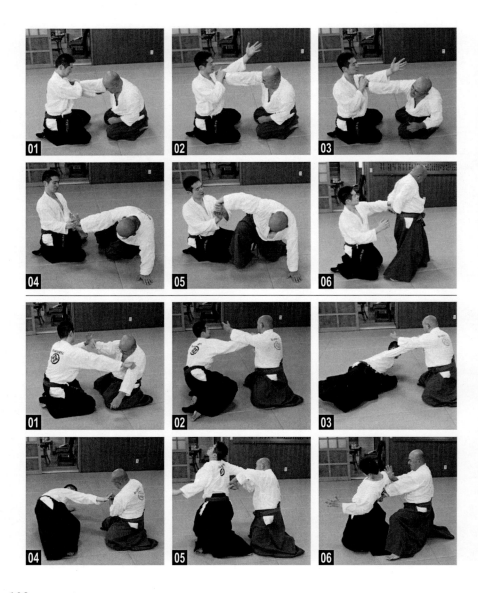

Chapter 10
One can only concentrate for a short time

Mune Osae Dori Mochi Mawari (Chest Pin Arrest Lead Around, 3rd Dan level)

This technique is similar to Ude Osae Dori Mochi Mawari on the previous. In this technique the opponent tries to grasp your chest instead of your upper arm. Then, you secure his right wrist using both hands to control and drop the opponent. Finally, you allow the opponent to rise up and then control him by turning him around (Mochi Mawari). In this case, the way of locking the wrist is not the same as the previous technique.

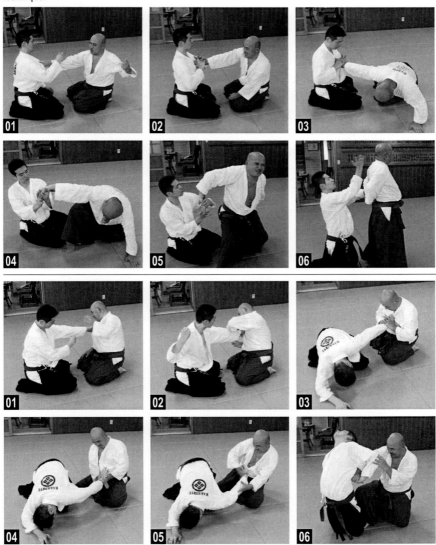

109

In fact, it took only 4 minutes to perform all 36 techniques. How extremely cohesive the performance was. Here, I should also mention that Okuyama 2nd Soke took on the role of Uke, which means he was thrown as well as executing the techniques himself. And he performed the role of Uke while receiving pain and being unbalanced. Thus, according to his reaction, I could recognise if the techniques that his partner was applying were effective or not.

Such a training method is seldom seen in other Budo forms. In most forms of Budo, they teach in a manner that allows students to try many different ways to perform techniques so they may discover for themselves the best way among their various trials. But, in Hakkoryu, they begin training by allowing students to experience the best way to perform techniques from the start.

Okuyama 2nd Soke says, "In Hakkoryu, we train our students by personal instruction, and not by group or mass teaching. There is no exception." I took his words as reasonable. Consequently, expert practitioners of the art pay close attention to lead the beginners in their execution of techniques.

On [photos 10-3], such instruction is shown where Okuyama 2nd Soke, as Uke, corrected Tori's arm positioning during the moment he is unbalanced by the technique, Ude Osae Dori (Arm Pin Art, 1st Dan level).

This happened in one instance during the 4 minutes when all the techniques were performed in a highly efficient manner, but I could still see their sincere teaching attitude when a very important point in the technique was corrected. It was a very impressive moment for me to witness this. Further, I was also impressed by the excellent completeness of the technical system itself.

I made the choice of techniques at random, but after putting them in a table, I noticed that all the techniques were related to each other from the lower to higher levels. This means that when you master one technique in a lower level, you already have a foundation prepared for the same technique in a higher level. The techniques are arranged in such a related sequence.

This relationship does not always correspond to level of difficulty. Please read the descriptions which are included on [photos 10-2] by their order, then you will understand what I have explained here as "they are related to each other".

Chapter 10
One can only concentrate for a short time

Ude Osae Dori
(Arm Pin Art, 2nd Dan level)

This Ude Osae Dori (2nd Dan level) technique is shown on [photos 10-2]. In this technique it is important where you hook your right arm over the opponent's left arm. It should be near his elbow but the location should be very precise, otherwise it does not work effectively.

In this case, Okuyama 2nd Soke detected that the location was slightly off, so he corrected his student by instructing, "Move it slightly to this side."

It is a unique feature of Hakkoryu to lead their students directly to the correct way of performing a technique without too many wrong attempts on their part. However, this can only be done through personal hands-on training, as demonstrated here.

photos 10-3

111

As a result you can make steady progress practicing one technique after another quite smoothly. The psychological effect is also significant in that you can master each step much easier than you may have expected.

At a glance, their way of training does not look very special, but several secrets are concealed in the curriculum, in that you can concentrate fully, and subsequently, master the techniques quite effectively and with sophistication. You may not notice these secrets with just a glance, because they may be quite simple and seem like normal details, but such details or aspects cannot often be performed easily.

◈ Requirement for concentration

In the other Ryu (traditions), it is common that the highest ranked teacher will never take the role of Uke. Or such a person will not even teach a beginner directly.

Considering this, I feel it is not polite to throw Okuyama 2nd Soke as Uke. I cannot help hesitating to feel this way. Maybe it is also an important point that they always smile during training, which helps eliminate such hesitation. With such smiling, they look like they really enjoy the training.

Besides, the Uke calls out with a "scream" when he feels real pain. They keep necessary seriousness continuously during training time and never lose their concentration. But, on the other hand, they make themselves free from unnecessary tension. This must be a feature of Hakkoryu's and also the headmaster's ability and character.

It is necessary to arrange the proper conditions to realise true concentration. In that way, Hakkoryu's training system is excellent and well organised. It is excellent in the point that they eliminate unnecessary aspects which inhibit their progress.

Reflecting on this myself, I am in too much distress over so many unnecessary and unimportant matters in my daily life. So, should I try to eliminate these through a dedicated and fully concentrated 20 minutes each day?

I am curious what I can do in those 20 minutes today.

Chapter 10
One can only concentrate for a short time

Chapter 11

The technique of guiding your opponent to do what you intend

◈ Guide the opponent to his defeat

There is one main theory in Hakkoryu which convinces us that it may be the strongest Bujutsu. This theory is: "The one who attempts action first shall lose." According to this theory you just try not to do anything to win. In fact, it is not that easy to employ this theory, but it sounds very simple, or I dare say, even too easy. If one will strike or grasp another, he will become unbalanced simply because of his intention to try to attack this person. On the contrary, if you can remain just as you are, avoiding becoming unbalanced in the situation in which you are attacked, then relatively speaking, you will not lose.

"Because Hakkoryu is a Goshinjutsu, you need it only when you encounter the situation of being attacked by another. There is no need to do anything on your side."

Perhaps Okuyama 2nd Soke has spoken this sentence a thousand times by now, but it resonates with deep meaning.

It is often said that you must "attack first to win", or "if you are the first to move you will win." If people believe this concept they cannot understand the responsive concept of Hakkoryu. But if you watch the fight from a third party's perspective, you might understand. The one who moves first, more or less unbalances himself because of the action he takes to attack. A similar concept is that by remaining still, you will never fall down.

Then all you have to do is just wait? In one sense "Yes, it is", but the words have a deeper technical concept which is concealed in the theory of Hakkoryu. This concept is that one should be "guiding the other's technique."

Chapter 11
The technique of guiding your opponent to do what you intend

Theory to lose if you start the action first
If one starts attacking by hitting or grasping the other, he shall always lose his balance through that action. The other who receives the attack can win by just keeping himself stable without being unbalanced. Then he can attain victory as a result.

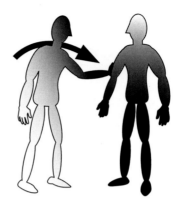

illustration 11-1

In Hakkoryu, there are no armed techniques. Considering it is a Goshinjutsu system, this is quite logic. However, there are some techniques in which everyday objects or tools are used, but they are not weapons.

On [photos 11-1], the usage of an umbrella is shown. The use of an umbrella may be viewed as being unrealistic by some, and even immediately looked down upon by many. However, please pay attention to its psychological effect, which is sophisticatedly concealed in this technique.

Okuyama 2nd Soke holds an open umbrella in front of his centre line.

If you are his opponent and you are confronted with this situation, you have no choice but to take away that umbrella or push it aside to create space for the attack. Namely, at that moment your action is unconsciously limited to approaching and dealing with the umbrella.

In this case, Okuyama 2nd Soke holds the umbrella in one hand, so you automatically think that you could easily overpower Okuyama 2nd Soke and take it away from him using both of your hands. Subsequently, you grasp the umbrella with both hands to force it away from Okuyama 2nd Soke.

"The point is not to resist. You just think about giving the umbrella to him."

It is important to guide him to take the above action. Until that moment, Okuyama 2nd Soke did nothing. It is only the opponent who took action. As indicated previously, by taking the first action, the opponent has unbalanced himself significantly, which has gone unnoticed by him because everything has gone as he intended. This "do as I want" or unchallenged situation accelerates his offensive action even further.

Kasa Osae Dori photos 11-1
(Umbrella Seize Art, Shihan/Okuden level)

When Okuyama 2nd Soke holds an umbrella to his front in a natural posture, the opponent tends to hold it unconsciously. Normally, he pulls back his grasping hands, then, Okuyama 2nd Soke steps forward by synchronising with this pulling action and applies Gakun to the opponent's left wrist (by which he holds the lower part of the umbrella). Okuyama 2nd Soke then pins the opponent down on the floor through the application of the Gakun.

In case the opponent pushes forward instead of pulling back, Okuyama 2nd Soke pulls back the umbrella by synchronising his own movement with the opponent's pushing motion. Okuyama 2nd Soke grasps the opponent's right wrist which the opponent used to grasp the upper part of the umbrella handle. Okuyama

In case of pulling back

Chapter 11
The technique of guiding your opponent to do what you intend

2nd Soke applies Gakun to his right wrist and raises that wrist high so he can step under and execute a throw.

In both cases, Okuyama 2nd Soke continues holding the umbrella until the very end, which is marvellous. He can finish in such a way because he succeeded in leading the opponent into taking the action in which he intended. At the moment the opponent was allowed to pull or push according to Okuyama 2nd Soke's intention, the result was already determined, or so it appears. Speaking of the Gakun, which Okuyama 2nd Soke used as a finish, it causes more pain in the case that the opponent puts more force in his arm/wrist. This is also a hidden technique in which to leverage the other's reaction.

In case of pushing forward

117

Although Okuyama 2nd Soke said his thoughts were only on handing the umbrella over, he doesn't actually do it. Okuyama 2nd Soke moves forward by synchronizing his movement with the opponent's action to pull the umbrella. In this situation the opponent grasps the umbrella with both hands and he is pulling it back. So he provides Okuyama 2nd Soke a great chance to control him. Hakkoryu has an especially effective technique that fits in such a situation. It is the Gakun.

The more the opponent puts power in his arm, the more pain he receives by this Gakun technique. This is such an awkward technique for an opponent. Okuyama 2nd Soke applied Gakun to the opponent and controlled him by pinning him to the floor. Okuyama 2nd Soke still continues holding the umbrella with one hand, which means Okuyama 2nd Soke has not lost his balance at all.

If the opponent pushes forward with both hands instead of pulling back, Okuyama 2nd Soke showed that variation as well, and it was fantastic. This variation is also formalized as a technique, which means such a situation is also within the plan. In this variation Okuyama 2nd Soke also does not resist the opponent's movement.

He steps back to synchronize with the opponent's forward pushing motion, and pulls back the umbrella to reinforce that movement. Then he applies Gakun to the opponent's right hand, which is located in front, and throws him down. In this technique, he also continues holding the umbrella with one hand.

It goes without saying that it is an extremely sophisticated technique to lead another to take the action in which you intend. It is almost impossible to do this unless you can manipulate their intent and convince them to believe it is through their own will that they do so.

"You can do it simply without resisting. If you do it naturally, the outcome automatically happens this way."

At first, when I heard Okuyama 2nd Soke explaining it through such plain words (while smiling) I thought it was a joke. But after watching his techniques and hearing his explanation several times, I have started thinking that it must be the ultimate, highest level expression of technique. If you can move naturally, the result should be clear. And Okuyama 2nd Soke can clearly forecast that outcome. But again, I must reiterate that it is quite

Chapter 11
The technique of guiding your opponent to do what you intend

difficult for us to behave naturally. We undeniably tend to make unnecessary or unnatural actions and accordingly, will lose our balance.

◉ Mystery of Continuing to Grasp

Mune Dori Nage (Chest Seizure Throw, Shihan/Okuden level), which is shown on [photos 11-2], might be the highest level technique in which to guide another.

Although it has the name of "Nage" (throw), one does not use their own hand for the throwing action. Does Okuyama 2nd Soke really throw the opponent? Okuyama 2nd Soke, in fact, let the opponent be thrown by their own actions.

When the opponent approached Okuyama 2nd Soke and grasped Okuyama 2nd Soke's training top around his chest, Okuyama 2nd Soke turned his upper body back in a slight motion, which resulted in the opponent having been thrown forward through the air.

The most fantastic aspect of this technique is that the opponent cannot release his grasping hands. When you watch this technique you surely doubt that this can be true, but if you try it yourself, you realize that you cannot release your hands. When you are thrown in such situation, you normally have the feeling that you are forced to do something by power. But in this technique you do not get this feeling at all, which is quite strange. Hence, you have no chance to release your hands. In other words, you do not have any problem keeping your grasp, and this is why you do not release your hands. That said, you cannot release your hands anyway.

Okuyama 2nd Soke's movement is actually rather large, as he turns his body 180-degrees, although he keeps the same distance. He carries out such a large motion without changing the tension the opponent feels in his grasping hands. That is why he does not feel anything strange or awkward with his grip and continues holding on.

If someone applies a movement or motion by which you do not feel their power, in a pulling or pushing manner for example, you cannot react to that motion and accordingly, you keep grasping with your hands unconsciously. As a result (in this technique), your arms cross over each other very unnaturally, which actually pins you with your own arms. Your only option to escape from this severe situation is to throw yourself forward. This technique is much more dangerous than it looks because the opponent cannot use his hands to take Ukemi, as they are still grasping the collars of the training jacket.

"When a person is attacked or forced to do something against their will, even it is a small attack or force, he tries to resist this unconsciously. Then it becomes a situation in which both struggle to gain power. This is not a technique to overpower the other by force."

I think the explanation Okuyama 2nd Soke gave this time has a much deeper meaning than simply saying "Do it without power."

He means that what makes the technique work is the other's motion and power rather than your own.

In the beginning of this chapter I described Hakkoryu as "the strongest Bujutsu", but I have to mention that they never actually say that themselves. I have been thinking that I seldom find such a Bujutsu as Hakkoryu that is as poor at self-promotion, or advertising art and expanding their organization.

Because they do not advertise or hold many public demonstrations, their activity is not well known to the public. Most people have no chance to see their techniques, but they have never struggled to survive as a Bujutsu.

"In Bujutsu, there is no need to declare that you are superior to all the others. Good Bujutsu always survives. No doubt about it."

Okuyama 2nd Soke knows very well that if one tries to devalue others, this shall inevitably take you down as a consequence. The best Bujutsu shall employ its finest influence in the case where others try to devalue it. There is no need to react to such defamation. Just leave it as they wish. If one can consider it in this way, they can gain stability in their mind and will not be easily agitated. We would probably describe such a situation as "self-confidence".

All of us have such experiences in our daily life that we become agitated by insignificant matters, such as rude comments from others, or possibly harassment, humiliation, or even having our own property stolen from us. We should not worry about such matters. Just leave them as they are. If you can only keep yourself resolute, the situation will surely turn to your favour.

Chapter 11
The technique of guiding your opponent to do what you intend

Mune Dori Nage photos 11-2
(Chest Seizure Throw, Shihan/Okuden level)

When the opponent grasps Okuyama 2nd Soke's collars with both hands, Okuyama 2nd Soke turns his body 180-degrees while raising his right arm. During this turning motion, Okuyama 2nd Soke keeps the distance between his chest and the front of the opponent's shoulders the same, then moves under and turns while sinking down, which gives the opponent no strange feeling of being forced something. By unconsciously continuing to maintain their grasp, the opponent's arms cross over each other, ending in a painful posture which compels the opponent to throw himself forward to escape from this severe locked position.

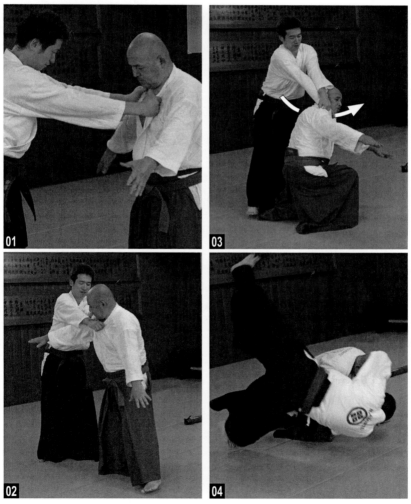

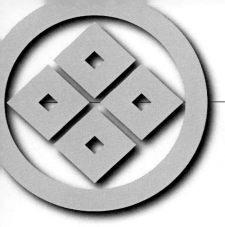

Chapter 12

Goshin Taiso (self-defense physical exercise)

◈ True enhancement activity for human beings

In Hakkoryu they have a program called Goshin Taiso (self-defense physical exercise). From its name I supposed it might be some exercise related to striking and kicking methods. But actually it is a self-training method.

Here, the important point is what is actually trained. In the case that one might build and strengthen all the muscles of the body, does it mean in the true sense, that they have become a strongman? I do not deny the importance of building muscle, but it should not be the entire purpose of physical exercise. In addition, I do not feel that strength training or body-building is necessarily good for self-defense training.

"Real self-defense training should also cover the mental aspect as well." Training focused only on the physical aspects cannot produce a complete self-defense system. Okuyama 2nd Soke relates that the founder had left the following words regarding physical exercise.

"Those physical exercises which have become popular nowadays, one focusing only on mental training, and the other focusing only on hardening the surface area of the human body—which is not related with viscera functions. Both inhibit the development of bringing the mind and body into harmony."

I know it is logical that having only one of these is not sufficient. Knowing this, people in modern times tend to think that the mind and body are independent. But in Hakkoryu, they regard mental effect—first and foremost—as the most important factor, and their reinforcement methods focus not only physical aspects, but on mental aspects as well.

Chapter 12
Goshin Taiso (self-defense physical exercise)

"It is important to strengthen the center (i.e., to cultivate one's courage which arises from abdomen). If one can train that strong courage, his motion becomes more rational, the circulatory system in one's body functions better, and accordingly, his mind becomes stable. This means that, in other words, the abdomen is the center of a human being's body."

It is a problem that we cannot find an appropriate method to reinforce power created within the abdomen in modern medicine. The spread of modern western medicine brought not only good things, but also bad things, I think. One of these bad things is that it caused many people to think that the mind and body are independent of each other.

Here, let's introduce more words from the founder.

"Our physical exercise aims to combine the base of the brainstem optic nerve, which functions as the center of all mental action, and the center part of both the back and the abdomen, which is the center of the body. This is accomplished through the assistance of physical reaction created by posturing, and both feet treading on the floor, in addition to the physical power created by the center of the abdomen, through the reciprocating motion of the diaphragm utilized for breathing. This should be the basis for all physical exercise, which becomes effective for practising all Hakkoryu techniques through the integration of mind and body."

This became the basic concept by which Goshin Taiso was established. It is a wonderful concept where they regard mind and body as being integrated as one, from the aspect of physics.

On [photos 12-1], this self-defense physical exercise (Goshin Taiso) is shown, comprising a total of 12 movements. One can diagnose how well one is functioning according to how well one can perform each movement. If one of the movements is not being performed well, then something should be wrong with the related body part or function.

If one continues this self-defense physical exercise, they become more sensitive to their health condition, and their sensitivity for potential health risk is improved. At this point I feel that this is a remarkable feature for a self-defense art.

Goshin Taiso photos 12-1
(self-defense physical exercise)

No. 1
Set both of your feet shoulder width apart. Cross your arms on your chest. Place your eyes straight forward naturally, without conscious thought. Raise you right leg to the front while you lean forward into your left knee a bit. Slowly tilt your upper body backwards. Execute Kiai with the sound of "Um" as in the first movement.
Corresponding disease: gastric ulcer, stomach cancer, expanding difficulty of all intestines and intestinal membrane, schizophrenic and light level neurosis.

No. 2
The motion continues right after exercise No. 1. Step forward with the right foot which you raised up in No 1, and stretch out your left leg that held your weight in the first exercise. Keep both of your arms crossed on your chest. At the moment you step forward your right foot, perform Kiai with the sound of "Um" while the mouth is closed.
Correspondence disease: eye disease, diabetes, and poor activity of the nutrition endocrine (i.e., which needs insulin dosage).

No. 3
Stand on your right leg only, while keeping your arms crossed on your chest. Slowly lean the upper body forward. Stretch your left leg backward and keep the chin as high as possible. Fix your eyes straight forward, and execute Kiai with the sound of "Um" as before.
Corresponding disease: gastric distension, gastric atony, dizziness caused by stiffness in the back, and gastrointestinal problems caused by overworking.

Chapter 12
Goshin Taiso (self-defense physical exercise)

One must practise all these 12 motions for both the right and left side. Each has a different motion, but in every motion you have to concentrate your force into your abdomen with Kiai (guttural verbalized exhalation, similar to a shout). Each motion has the effect to improve and heal problems related to the certain body part or functions. And if one has a problem related to a certain body part or function, he cannot perform the related motion well, and consequently, it is used as an indicator of one's health problem.

No. 4

This motion continues right after exercise No. 3. It starts immediately by raising your body upright and placing your right leg straight forward. Bend your left leg and make a strong stance backwards. Execute Kiai with the sound of "Um" while the mouth is closed.

Corresponding disease: gastric ulcer, duodenal ulcer, weakness, and poor vigour.

No. 5

Stand only on the left leg, while keeping the arms crossed on your chest. Lean the upper body to the left side and raise the right leg high to the side of your body. While doing this, keep your toes pointing upward and your upper body facing to the front with the eyes fixed straight forward. Execute Kiai with the sound of "Um" as before.

Corresponding disease: poor ability to think and memory loss, rough skin condition that is chapped and/or cracked, and hearing loss.

No. 6

This motion continues right after exercise No. 5. Place the raised right leg forward to your front while straightening your upper body. During this motion, you continue to keep the eyes fixed straight forward. Step slightly to the right front oblique with the right foot and grip the floor strongly as if you will kick through the floor. Execute Kiai with the sound of "Um" as in the preceding movements.

Corresponding disease: poor functioning of all intestines, liver disorder, prevention and care of herniated disk, menorrhagia, prevention of hemophilia and scurvy.

125

No. 7

This continues from exercise No. 6. Stretch both arms straight up while gripping the floor with both heels, which are placed close together. At the moment you stretch up both arms, perform Kiai with the sound of "Um" while the mouth is closed.

Corresponding disease: lowering all viscera caused by weak intestinal membrane.

No. 8

From No. 7, you immediately step forward with the right foot and drop down your right hand to the front of the right shoulder, while keeping the right elbow tucked tightly to the side of your body. Pull the right hand toward the right shoulder using the left hand, which is holding the right hand from above.
Corresponding disease: all intestinal problems caused by weakened activity of the blood metabolism, tumor, and a person who easily gets hives.

No. 9

Grip the floor with both heels and, using this force, stretch both arms behind your body and maintain this posture while bending your head backwards and looking straight up toward the ceiling. Fully stretch the hips and push out your chest, while contracting, or clenching your belly.
Corresponding disease: chronic intestinal disorder, malnutrition caused by poor absorbing function of the small intestine, obesity, and being too emaciated (skinny).

Chapter 12
Goshin Taiso (self-defense physical exercise)

No. 10

From No. 9, you immediately pull back your right foot and grip the floor. Make a fist with the right hand and pull the right elbow close to the side of the body. Try to pull the right fist towards your body, while the left hand restricts this motion from the inside (between the right fist and body). With this motion, you train the right arm's pulling power. Contract, or clench the muscles on the inside of the upper and lower right arm.
Corresponding disease: weak cardiac function, abnormal blood pressure, vertigo, neuralgia, rheumatism, arthritis, etc.

No. 11

Grip the floor strongly with both heels, and using this impulse force reaction, open both arms wide to each side of the body. Then twist both arms slightly backwards.
Corresponding disease: problems with intestinal membranes, such as peritoneum pleural, pleura, endometrium, perimetrium, and autonomic imbalance caused by dislocation of intestines.

No. 12

From No. 11, step forward with your right foot. Make a fist in the left hand and lower it behind your back. Raise the right hand up while making a fist and rotate it up and over your right shoulder. Execute Kiai with the sound of "Um" while the mouth is closed.
Corresponding disease: various problems caused by uncontrollable adjustment of metabolism of carbon dioxide gas and blood circulation, and the prevention of myocardial infarction.

❀ How to reach into the "center"

In each motion there is a concentration within the abdomen (midpoint between the hips and belly) with a Kiai (guttural verbalized exhalation, similar to a shout) and treading of the feet on the floor.

There is hidden knowledge in how to execute these physical exercises effectively, which looks easy if you regard it as such. It is posturing.

If we say abdomen, then we tend to focus only on the belly, or front side of the body. In such a case, we only tend to contract mainly the rectus abdominis muscles. In simpler terms, we had better also expand the muscles on the back the same as we contract the rectus abdominis muscles. You should create good alignment by placing the hips forward and straightening your back bone (refer to [photos 12-2]).

You will discover a big difference when using this action and without. I asked Okuyama 2nd Soke for additional clarification because this is such an important matter. The abdomen is located inside the human body, and accordingly, a person who is not sensitive might have difficulty realizing where the abdomen is. "Is there a good way to realize it easier?"

For this question, Okawa Shihan replied by saying "Though this is just my own idea…. Speaking to "concentration", I have an image that an object is expanding and in that center, there exists a substance with a large mass, like a bowling ball."

Hmmm, I think I can understand what he is saying. If you have a mental image of a substance that expands instead of shrinks, then its center becomes recognized clearer.

Also that image makes it clear that there is no separation between the actions of contracting the belly and stretching the back.

This Goshin Taiso itself can be practised by everyone as a means of health maintenance. But for those people who practise Hakkoryu, its practise is leveraged to master the usage of body center, which directly related to the development of techniques.

For example, in the first movement, it is rather hard to lean your upper body backwards standing on one leg, if you do it without paying careful attention. But if you pay attention to set your hips forward to establish a stable body center, you can do it with good balance and it is much easier. It

Chapter 12
Goshin Taiso (self-defense physical exercise)

It is possible to make a centering of the posture that has no deviation between the belly and back through a fine tuning adjustment of your posture. You can achieve this centering by creating the proper posture while setting your upper hip forward and raising your pelvis up.

By creating this posture, you can eliminate power deviation over the surface of the body, and attain overall stability that is established by the core of the body. If you compare the two photos without enough knowledge, it is not easy to notice the difference in posture. This is because you tend to focus on the location of the head or angle of the backbone to the floor. They both look similar, but there is actually a huge difference. Please pay attention to the angle of the black belt. The superiority of the correct posture shown in the second photo is the same in both performing techniques, and in daily life. In addition, it has a tremendous benefit to bring about stability in the mind.

photos 12-2

is important in the practice of Hakkoryu techniques to learn how to make correct posturing through the practise of these physical exercises.

It is important that you keep correct posture. But of course you cannot keep such ideal natural posturing for 24-hours a day. However, if you awaken your body center correctly you can maintain good balance in any position. The stability which you attain through these physical exercises means both the physical stability of the body when you perform the techniques, as well as the strength of mental stability in which to deal with your daily problems. If you can keep good mental stability in any crisis situation, there is nothing you will fear in this world. That is "self-defense" in your mind.

There is another remarkable and excellent point to this Goshin Taiso which many of the readers might have noticed. All these 12 motions are actually related to 12 meridians of the human body, in the following manner:

No 1. Expanding function of all intestines; center stomach meridian
No 2. Nutrition endocrine function; center spleen meridian
No 3. Shrinking function of all intestines; center urinary bladder meridian
No 4. Reproduction endocrine function; center kidney meridian
No 5. Expanding and shrinking adjustment function; center gallbladder meridian
No 6. Reproduction and nutrition adjustment function; center liver meridian
No 7. Raising all intestinal (viscera) function; center large intestine meridian
No 8. Blood metabolism function; center lung meridian
No 9. All intestinal movement function; center small intestine meridian
No10. Blood circulation function; center heart meridian
No11. Raising and hauling adjustment function; center triple Energizer Meridian
No12. Metabolism and circulation adjustment function; center percardium Meridian

When I line up those 12, I notice they cover all meridians uniformly and all consist of the key word "center".

There is still not a clear answer to the question "Where is the spirit?"

Nowadays, the foremost answer is "It exists in the brain." But in my opinion the answer which fits best is, "It exists in the abdomen."

In case of an emergency situation, it will not help to keep a cool head using an ice bag, but if one can do something with his abdomen, it will surely help recover a sense of calmness.

The founder said the following.

"If one can succeed in uniting each central part of the body and mind related to each other, and therefore become stronger, the following good wills as sincerity for sake of one's benefit, loyalty to society, pure love, clear mind, good alignment, good sense, and fighting spirit for justice at

Chapter 12
Goshin Taiso (self-defense physical exercise)

the risk of his own life, will surely be generated from inside of the person. The ideal goal of our physical exercise can be explained in plain words as a training method so that one can align both centers of mind and body. Accordingly, I believe all education should be based on such proper physical exercise."

His declaration does not sound like an irrational argument at all. In Japan, all the junior high schools are now obliged to implement some Budo program in their educational curriculum. But I wonder, and doubt, if the persons responsible for this in those schools have such a deep consideration regarding their Budo education programs.

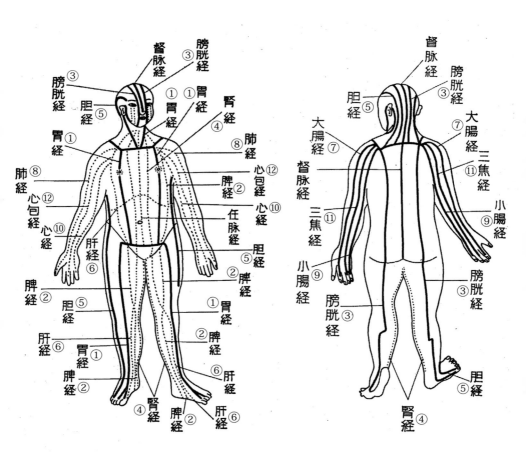

Chapter 13

The teaching contained in escaping from a bound rope

◈ Secret technique of Nawa Nuke (Rope Escape)

You surely wonder and doubt what is going on when you look at [photos 3-1]. This is the secret technique of Nawa Nuke (Rope Escape, Okuden level) of Hakkoryu. I was really surprised indeed to know that they have such a technique.

Regarding this Nawa Nuke, everybody probably questions why such a technique is included in a Jujutsu system.

"It does not happen often that somebody would have a use for this technique, but it has a certain meaning in which to master such escape techniques. Even in such a situation where everyone would normally give up and abandon their effort to overcome, the fact one mastered this technique gives them confidence to overcome. It has such a mental effect."

Having heard Okuyama 2nd Soke's explanation, I though it made sense. It is a practical technique, but it also has a good mental effect, which is a special feature of Hakkoryu. But is it really possible to escape from a bound rope? You never know which way you will be bound by a rope in a real situation.

"No problem. You have to think that this is not a technique to untie, or unbind a rope, but to escape from a bound rope. The point is escaping. Normally, people try to unbind the rope, in which case, they are led into a dead end. But if you aim to escape from a bound rope, there is a way. Because the human body cannot be locked ridged, or in other words, if your body became locked solid, there would be no hope. The most important point in this chapter is how to make your body relaxed."

Chapter 13
The teaching contained in escaping from a bound rope

Nawa Nuke   photos 13-1
(Rope escape, Shihan level, Okuden)

In this technique of Nawa Nuke, one escapes from being bound by both of his wrists with a tight rope. It is important not to try to unbind a rope, but to escape from a rope. The key for success is how one can wholly relax himself. Because the rope is bound as tightly as possible, if one uses even a tiny degree of power, then the technique does not work at all. But, if you can totally relax yourself you can find a way to escape from whatever way you are bound. That is the point.

01

02

In fact, this case (bound in the front) is much more difficult than being bound behind the back. Because you can see the place where you are bound, then you tend to put force there unconsciously.

133

◈ Do not watch the bound rope!

So, Okuyama 2nd Soke showed me the technique itself. He was bound quite tightly with both his hands behind his back. If I was him, I would surely have given up any attempt to escape from it.

Then Okuyama 2nd Soke freed his hands from the bound rope, which took no longer than one minute. We often watch similar performances in magic shows, but this was no trick.

Because his movement was so small, I could not recognize what happened, but because of his prior explanation I could guess, and understood what was going on. He relaxed and abandoned force in his arms, then he reduced the friction, or contact between the rope and the skin of his arms as much as possible. He then moved his arms little by little. However, he was bound so tightly that he could not overcome the frictional force that easily.

"That is why you need to abandon your force completely. It is one of our basic concepts to reduce unnecessary force from your body. And especially for this technique, it is absolutely essential to realize that concept very firmly."

The threshold of whether you can complete this technique or not is at quite a high level. Even a tiny residual force in your arms might cause the failure of this technique.

"In that sense it becomes more difficult if your wrists are bound in front of you."

It is because in this case you can see your bound hands or arms, and it causes you to become conscious of it, and even a small degree of consciousness makes your arms stiff and that results in failure. What a delicate matter it is!

When Okuyama 2nd Soke was bound with his hands behind his back, I thought it would be impossible for him to escape. Everybody might agree. But the real solution exists in a totally different place, like in a different dimensional space.

"You should not comprehend the phenomenon superficially. You should leverage more general sense, which is much more important. For instance, in case you had to fight against multiple enemies, you will be defeated if you try

Chapter 13
The teaching contained in escaping from a bound rope

to watch the opponents one by one in order to judge how to respond, then your reaction shall occur too late."

After hearing this I remembered one amazing performance that had taken place at the Shihan's demonstration that I previously attended. One of the highest ranked Deshi (student) from the founder's period, Matsumoto Shihan, performed his techniques without watching the attacker's movement at all.

This is also Hakkoryu's remarkable feature, to achieve Kime (final control) in an instant. This is often regarded as the result of the high-level and completeness of the techniques, but more likely, it is the result of their speed in sensing the attacker's movement.

The essence of this is described by the words "eyes to watch generally", in other words, to see everything but not focus only on a small part, requires a certain sense. The way in which to improve that sense seems to be implemented in this Nawa Nuke technique.

Here Okuyama 2nd Soke showed me another technique. Without seeing his two opponents that attack Okuyama 2nd Soke from behind, he pushed them down to his rear under his back. I immediately thought it must be an ultra-high-level technique, given that he could control the opponents in such a posture. But, Okuyama 2nd Soke told me without using any words, just

This Futari Dori is a miracle technique. Okuyama 2nd Soke controls two opponents behind his back who attack him from the rear. For techniques like this with multiple attackers, once you focus only on one person, then you are brought to a standstill and the technique does not work.

photos 13-2

with the look in his eyes "That way of thinking is wrong." Yes, indeed, I fixated on only what I saw in the same way I became fixed when I saw Nawa Nuke. For me it seemed to be a hopeless situation as that one is bound with both hands behind the back.

◈ Elaborate skills in the hands

The technique Nawa Nuke has several Kuden (verbal teachings) and Yoketsu (secret keys). All of them cannot be introduced here but, one of them is: "It is the teaching that you perform Nawa Nuke as if you are applying Gakun to your own wrist."

As already explained in the previous chapter, Gakun produces unbearable pain to the opponent and can control him with only a light grasping power on the opponent's wrist. This is one on the representative techniques of Hakkoryu. If you are on the receiving end of the Gakun, you receive enormous pain and cannot continue standing in good posture due to that pain.

At a glance it looks like one just holds and grasps the opponent's wrist lightly, and it was a mystery why the opponent received sharp pain by such a light grasp. After watching the techniques several times I started understanding that the techniques work due to elaborate skills. Of course, you should not grip strongly. It is the same as Nawa Nuke, in that you have to abandon force from within your arm/hand. The Kake (defender) should give up force to succeed, and Uke (attacker) receives intense pain if he puts force into his arm/wrist. So, one must perform both roles by themselves to realize this Nawa Nuke technique successfully.

"It is important that you should not move the elbow. You often tend to move your elbow in a big motion, but then you cannot escape from the bound rope. You tighten both sides of the body and operate your hands precisely to release your bound wrists little by little. The movement is the same for Gakun. For Gakun, if you move your elbow, you surely try to use force, and in such a way, the Gakun does not work at all. For Gakun, you set your elbow as close as you can to the side of your body—and keep still—then you apply your body-weight into your grasping hand, not physically, but just through your imagination or mental intent.

The process of how to apply body weight is indescribably exquisite. That

Chapter 13
The teaching contained in escaping from a bound rope

Gakun photos 13-3
(Shihan level of 3rd Dan Waza)

This technique starts with your action to hold the opponent's wrist. It looks as if you bend the opponent's wrist using the power of your hand/arm, but actually not. You do not use that much muscular force for this technique. Being grasped by their own wrist, the opponent puts force into their wrist reactively and it results in tension, which causes them enormous pain. You can leverage this pain to control him. Therefore, in theory, if the opponent could keep relaxed in this situation, as if his wrist was not grasped, this technique could not work. But for normal unexperienced people it is impossible. The important know how of this technique is described below.

Keep your elbow close to your body, and fix that location during the motion.

Abandon force from the arm/hand and try to apply your arm weight to the opponent's wrist.

137

point was unknown to me and I did not notice it at all, although I have watched Gakun several times before this moment. This time Okuyama 2nd Soke explained to me one new point that I could not have figured out by myself. But, thanks to Okuyama 2nd Soke's kind explanation, I learned that it was "70-30% power allocation" (refer to [illustrations 13-1]).

Again I was so surprised that such an elaborate operation was done by hand. It is often said that one cannot understand what is done only by watching in Hakkoryu. It is surely the case for this Gakun because simple replication of the sequence does not work at all. Gakun has such elaborate skill, and with that elaboration, Gakun even makes it possible to escape from a bound rope. It is important not to be tense, which is the biggest precondition to realise such techniques. The three main Hakkoryu principles of "no challenge, no resistance and no injury" are applicable to this Nawa Nuke technique, which is wonderful.

Here, I wonder if I can apply these principles of no challenge and no resistance to an inanimate

Exquisite 70-30% allocation

It requires a quite delicate and exquisite means to apply your arm weight to the opponent's wrist. First you apply 70% of your arm weight straight down in the vertical direction. Then, keeping this 70% allocation of weight, apply the remaining 30% of your arm weight to the opponent's arm in the direction from their wrist to elbow. By this weight allocation, the Gakun works. If you become tense or stiff you, could never perform such a delicate action.

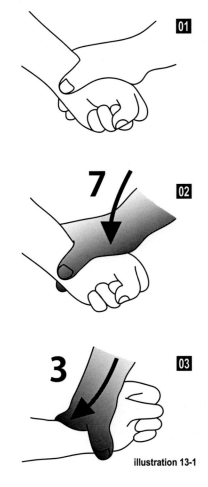

illustration 13-1

Chapter 13
The teaching contained in escaping from a bound rope

object, such as rope. It seems like an extremely difficult thing for me. Of course, it is already difficult enough to apply those principles to a person who is attacking me, but it seems much more difficult to do it against the rope, which binds me.

It does not matter in which situation you may find yourself, or against which opponent, you should always keep your action based on the principles. The founder, the 1st Soke (Shodai Soke), might have included the technique of Nawa Nuke in Hakkoryu's curriculum to implement such intention.

If we view this Nawa Nuke technique from the viewpoint of mental effect, which is the main theme of this book, we can understand that the technique provides us with a deep hint.

If one becomes in a hurry to resolve the predicament of the bound rope, one can never make it. First we have to accept facing the problem and do not resist it. If we can keep ourselves relaxed, we can move naturally—as we should do—and can overcome the problem.

We tell ourselves not to hurry and to keep a stable mind. Such situations often happen in our daily life. And it sometimes makes us even more hurried. It is because we try to force ourselves to become calm unconsciously, which we cannot realize easily, and that situation works negatively.

Do not resist and just accept the situation. That should be enough. If you do not worry yourself in vain, you can escape from the bound rope even without realizing you are succeeding in doing so.

Okuyama 2nd Soke performed an ultra-high-level and difficult technique, called Karada Mae Shibori (bound in front). He can escape from even such a difficult situation as this. If you can relax yourself, you can always find a way.

photo 13-4

Chapter 14

Resuscitation Methods

⬥ What we can learn from resuscitation methods

One time I was so startled to have heard something Okuyama 2nd Soke said to me: "In the case that someone is murdered, their iris drops down inside their eyeball. Conversely, in the case of suicide by hanging, the iris goes up."

Many of the readers might wonder why I would be startled by this, but I simply felt shock with the degree of his enormous level of knowledge. You could never find this information by searching the internet. One can only gather such knowledge and create techniques by following the ancient compiled knowledge and the standard rule of thumb. A Bujutsu should have been established based on the accumulation of such deep knowledge regarding the human body.

Here, I described it as "based on piled-up experiences", but in modern times, when we should have been able to compile a maximum degree of knowledge, what is our real level now? Regarding our current knowledge of the human body, we might have the poorest level of understanding throughout our history. Just as an example, in the case where we may encounter a person injured in a traffic accident, or a person who suddenly became ill, we might end up flustered and not know what to do. I recently encountered such a situation myself. I saw an elderly man fall down on the pavement that was crowded with pedestrians. In the moment of finding him, I could not do anything for him. No one else who was there could do anything either. All the people there were equally as flustered.

"Of course, in many cases like this, you should not move or even touch such a person. For instance, in the situation of a traffic accident, in most of

Chapter 14
Resuscitation Methods

the cases you should not move the injured person. In this instance, I would only measure his pulse."

That is the basic medical treatment contained within the Koho Shiatsu of Hakkoryu. This is a very high level technique in which one can check the whole body's condition just by measuring the pulse, or heart rate, of one's wrist.

In such a situation as described above, a person who has no knowledge of a treatment technique such as this should call an ambulance or the assistance of another with such knowledge. By the way, recently AED units (Automatic Extracorporeal Defibrillators) have been installed in train stations, or in other public facilities, which means the demand has been increasing for untrained people to provide emergency assistance. In addition, the resuscitation ratio without using an AED decreases 7-10 percent for each minute that passes without treatment.

"For example, in the case that someone attempted suicide by hanging, there is a possibility of successful resuscitation if begun within 5 minutes of the act."

In Hakkoryu, besides Koho Shiatsu, additional resuscitation methods are included in its curriculum. Students learn these resuscitation methods in the Okuden teachings of Shihan level. Okuyama 2nd Soke demonstrated one of these as an example.

"There is knowledge of how to raise up the another's upper body. First, roll the other person a little bit so that you can gain enough clearance between the floor and their back to put your knee in there. Then, place your arm under their neck and hold their opposite side shoulder, while your other hand holds their chin. Then, from that position, if you slowly pull up both hands/arms you can easily raise them up. It is a rather difficult task just to lift up someone else's upper body. If one does not know the proper way, and just tries to quickly lift up someone's upper body using force, they will likely fail. In such a case, first cross their arms in front of their chest—which puts their body in one large bunch and makes it significantly easier to move them. Also, this posture produces a mental effect that unconsciously gives one a sense of security."

Indeed, the process described can control another quite well as a technique taught in a Bujutsu curriculum.

141

Kappo photos 14-1
(Resuscitation Methods, Shihan/Okuden level)

Raising Another Person

First, roll the other a little bit so that you can get enough clearance between the floor and their back to put your knee in between. Next, hold the person's chin with your left hand. Then, put your right arm under their neck and hold their opposite shoulder while your other hand continues holding their chin. Finally, from that position, slowly pull up both ands/arms to raise the person.

Chapter 14
Resuscitation Methods

Resuscitation #1

Put both hands under each armpit of the person whose upper body you previously raised. Place your right knee on the centre-line of their back at the height of their Obi, or belt. While raising up and pulling back on both underarm's of the person, press forward into their back with your right knee.

143

Resuscitation #2

In case resuscitation #1 does not work, allow the person to lay down flat on their back with their chest open. Place both of their hands/arms on their chest and hold them. Synchronizing your breathing to theirs, slide both of their held hands from chest to belly while breathing out. You should repeat this motion at least 20-30 times. Then, while holding both of their hands with your left hand only, flick your right finger against their right cheek bone. It gives the person a sense of security to continue holding both of their hands on their chest.

Chapter 14
Resuscitation Methods

Considering those points, martial arts and medicine seem related to each other and not in separate categories. But resuscitation has a much deeper meaning in martial arts.

"In the case of raising someone, there is a difference between just executing the technical sequence and really trying to help someone. Of course, in the case of the later, this is much better. In the same way, with all the techniques of Hakkoryu, you should not apply them with the intention to simply execute them better. There are three main principles in Hakkoryu: no challenge, no resistance and no injury. As a result, the concept of resuscitation fulfils all three of these principles."

Yes, that is right. In resuscitation techniques, there is no rivalry. Okuyama 2nd Soke instructs that one should apply the martial arts techniques in the same mental state.

◉ Save a drowned person

The typical emergency situation that requires the quickest reaction is the resuscitation of a drowned person.

"The first action you have to do is expel the water. This might be unexpectedly difficult for a person who is not used to this action."

Okuyama 2nd Soke first showed us the proper way to skilfully use the knee to let a person vomit water (refer to [photos 14-2]). Here, the important point is to use Shiatsu to massage the stomach. He applied sharp stimulation on the exact points of the Koho Shiatsu method so well that Mr. Okawa, who took on the role of the victim, appeared likely to actually vomit.

By watching those actions, I observed that one should understand the anatomy of the human body well enough to practise resuscitation. These resuscitation methods and the techniques are the same in the sense that they cannot be practised by just form alone.

Okuyama 2nd Soke showed us another method of resuscitation by stimulating the meridians of the person who is now lying flat on their back (refer to [photos 14-3]). This looks like an easier posture and Okuyama 2nd Soke does this with a special rhythm. Also, he seems like he is not just pressing on the surface of the body, but his pressing makes a deeper connection on the inside of the body. Perhaps Okuyama 2nd Soke can "see" what he cannot

145

visually see with his eyes—probably by sensing or "seeing" mentally.

Frankly speaking, I do not understand why such resuscitation methods have not become more popular. I do not think I am over-exaggerating by saying that it is so important whether or not one's life could be saved in a critical situation, that every genre of martial arts should include such resuscitation methods, shouldn't they? We can certainly say this for sports, but also for general fighting techniques. If people try to practise choking techniques without anybody who knows resuscitation methods, it would be quite dangerous practise.

If anyone who does not know how to reassemble something plays with a puzzle, it is just dismantling and destroying. However, if one knows how to reassemble the pieces, one can carry on their disassembling work with the knowledge of how to reverse things and reassemble everything again. This should also apply to the original techniques of Bujutsu.

Here again I have to mention mental effect. Anger, hatred, attack, destruction—which are inherent aspects of Bujutsu—are also the strongest limitations to one's development. Those should be eliminated.

I ask myself how much I do to serve others and assist them in becoming more revitalized in society and in their daily life—or even if I have lost such an aspiration?

Those aspects that we appear to have been losing in our modern lives', they assuredly preserve in Hakkoryu.

Chapter 14
Resuscitation Methods

How to resuscitate a person who has drowned
photos 14-2
(how to expel the ingested water)

Position the person onto your right knee in a prone posture so that your right knee touches their belly and keeps their body bent. Massage their stomach firmly with the fingers of the left hand to induce vomiting.

Rub their body from chest to belly while pressing strongly. After repeating this motion 20 times, press on their lower stomach sharply, which causes a shock to resuscitation with a vomiting reaction. **photos 14-3**

Chapter 14
Resuscitation Methods

Chapter 15

Never do it too much

◉ Never make your own arrangement

The photo ([photo 15-1]) shows Kogan Shibori (Testicle Squeeze) from the Okuden section of the Kaiden teachings. Here the opponent's right arm controls his left arm and his right arm clinches his testicles (already introduced on [photos 0-5]).

Here we show the procedures of how you can get to this final stage. Please watch the continuous photo sequence shown on [photos 15-2]. As you can see there are many steps to this technique.

photo 15-1

Chapter 15
Never do it too much

photos 15-2

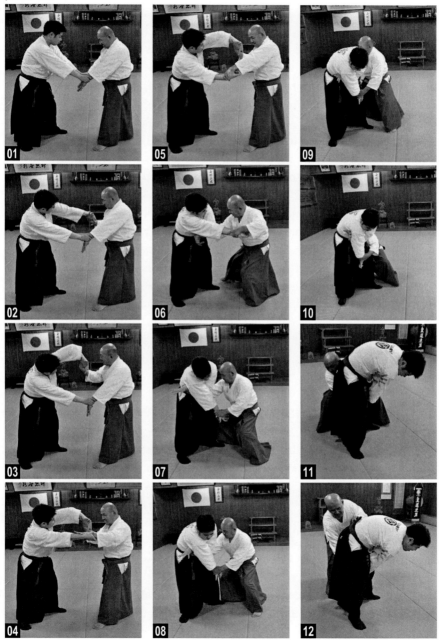

"When you look at these photos you tend to misunderstand what is going on and tend to think that you can very easily direct the opponent as you wish, which is not true. All the movements shown in this technique have a necessity to be applied, which means that you do not move the other freely as you may wish, rather the opponent moves by himself. This is a technique to allow the opponent to move in the pre-arranged way by himself" says Okuyama 2nd Soke.

I probably misunderstood this point myself. In Hakkoryu, they have several techniques in which they can unbalance others just by lightly touching them. Therefore, I did not think it would be difficult to move others freely, at will.

"Our Hakkoryu techniques can be executed with several different technical methods, but you should not change the techniques, or add any unnecessary movements to them (i.e., you should not make your own arrangement for these techniques). It is natural that one tends to think about making changes to the technical sequence, but if they do so, the technique loses its essence. If one does not understand the most important part of the technique (its essence), they tend to overdo some movements."

Okuyama 2nd Soke showed me an example for such a case with the technique of Tekagami (Hand Mirror, 1st Dan level) which we have already seen several times.

◈ Multiple unbalancing

"If I exaggerative a little bit here and say that one should not perform any action according to Hakkoryu's basic principles of no challenge, no resistance and no injury. But, so far as you want to apply a technique, you tend to do some active motion. We do have this dilemma in our techniques. In Tekagami (shown in the photos on [photos 15-3]) you should hold the opponent's wrist and cut the opponent's grasping hand using your Shuto (knife-hand) to throw him. In the case that you pay too much attention to your controlling of his wrist, you do this action too much. Then the technique does not work well, and as a result, you unbalance yourself. In fact, the unbalancing of the opponent should have been done in an earlier stage of the technique before cutting down on his hand."

Chapter 15
Never do it too much

Okuyama 2nd Soke raised his grasped left wrist without putting force into his left arm/hand, and then secured the opponent's right hand from underneath (which is grasping Okuyama 2nd Soke's left wrist) with his own right hand.

"Now, I can unbalance him. If I do it like this you will see it."

Saying this, Okuyama 2nd Soke pulled down both of his hands a little bit. The opponent then immediately started becoming unbalanced. Although his right hand was locked, somehow it did not look as if he was being controlled by the wrist lock.

"It is important that you should position both of your hands into the front centre of your body. Then, when the opponent tries to grasp your wrists, he starts unbalancing himself. Also, you drop down both your hands—not by power—but by the weight of your arms, with the assistance of gravity."

If you look back at this technique in which Okuyama 2nd Soke demonstrated, you will notice the only action Okuyama 2nd Soke made is that he raised his grasped left hand.

"You cannot throw the opponent by only twisting his wrist and cutting it with Shuto. In the case that you do not understand this, you start trying to twist his hand using your power. This is an example of overdoing it."

I also want to especially draw your attention to the fact that Okuyama 2nd Soke did not move a single step during the application of this technique. Because he did not move, he did not become unbalanced.

"Adding further explanation, the unbalancing of the opponent started at an earlier stage of the technique. At first, the opponent grasps your wrists and he pushes them. If you resist his pushing, then it becomes a power struggle which you do not have to engage in. You do not need to do anything but just leverage the weight of your arms, which can create enough stability as to not be easily pushed. In a case where he may push with even stronger power, please let him do so. The result is that he will lose his own balance by that action. So, in the strictest sense, his unbalancing starts from the very beginning."

This was quite a surprise to me. The unbalancing action has such multiple layers in this technique. You never even notice that the opponent started becoming unbalanced from the exact moment he grasped your wrist. That is why, if you do not notice this important fact, you tend to unbalance the

153

Tekagami   photos 15-3
(Hand Mirror, 1st Dan level)

At the moment you are grabbed by both wrists, you raise your grasped left hand as if you look at yourself in a compact mirror (Tekagami). Secure the opponent's right hand from underneath with your own right hand, then transfer your left arm's weight to the opponent's right hand. Release your grasped left wrist while continuing to control the opponent's right wrist with your right hand grip. Over the top of the opponent's grasped right hand, apply a left hand Shuto with a downward cutting motion to throw the opponent on your left side.

Chapter 15
Never do it too much

At the last stage, you throw the opponent not by twisting his wrist, nor pushing down on it, but by just placing the weight of your left arm onto his right arm. It is important to keep the point of action in front of your body's centre.

opponent by just twisting his wrist. If you attempt to do anything to make your control more certain through the implementation of stronger technique (which appears to be more effective), this actually makes the technique lose its essential element. That is the irony.

◈ "Never do too much" to restrict the opponent's freedom of movement

On [photos 15-4], the photos show Konoha Gaeshi (Leaf Turnover, 2nd Dan level).

Here, Okuyama 2nd Soke blocks the opponent's Jodan Tsuki (high thrust punch) with Shuto while not moving from his original standing position. He applies an unbalancing movement to affect the opponent only through a transfer of his weight. There is no tension in his body. It appears like he does nothing.

Please carefully study the last photo, No. 7. Here, Okuyama 2nd Soke controls only the opponent's right hand and the rest of the opponent's body is totally free. From this situation the opponent might make a counter-attack against Okuyama 2nd Soke by kicking, or he can resist by moving around aggressively. But, it seems like a miracle that he cannot move from this posture at all.

"If you can control the meridian of the large intestine, which starts at the index finger and goes through the palm side of a hand, the opponent loses his freedom of movement and cannot kick back at you. On the contrary, if you try to bend his hand with power, he can easily change the angle of his bent wrist and can recover freedom of movement. This technique will work if you perform only the motion necessary, but never too much."

I thought it must be a conflict in one's mind. If you are not confident in your ability to control the opponent only with one hand grasping, you tend to try to physically control the opponent with strength as a supplement. Because of your anxiety, you add such supplemental actions, one after another, which results in the technique being less and less effective.

If you can mentally overcome this unconfident situation, you can redirect yourself into the higher technical dimension. Or, because you could physically sublimate yourself to the higher technical dimension, you can be men-

Chapter 15
Never do it too much

tally free from such anxiety and/or being unconfident?

This concept as a mental teaching of "never overdo", might have redirected a Bujutsu to the same level of higher technical dimension. In the very old days of the Warring States Period, or Sengoku Jidai, when the origin of Bujutsu first began, its purpose was to defeat the enemy completely, so that they could no longer antagonize you. That is why attacking should be done powerfully and in the most direct and clear manner. A Bujutsu was used to realize such purpose at that time.

But in modern times, there is such a concept as "over defence". Even while defending yourself you should not excessively injure the attacker. If you breach this rule, you yourself will likely be criminally punished. In modern times, people have noticed the importance of this concept as "never overdo".

Thanks to Hakkoryu, we now have a much smarter alternative to defend ourselves with the concept of "never overdo", which has a miraculous effect to control the opponent who attacks you in a violent way.

Although the concept of "to do until the very end" carries some attraction, we cannot help feeling a margin of our mind with incomparably higher level or bigger capacity than that in the first case. Especially for a Bujutsu with the belief of "never overdo", we have the sense that such a Bujutsu is closer to ourselves and naturally easier to master.

For instance, if you are told by your boss "don't work too hard", instead of "work as hard as you can", most likely you will make up your mind to work harder.

Konoha Gaeshi photos 15-4
(Leaf Turnover, 2nd Dan level)

You block the opponent's right Jodan Tsuki with a left Shuto Barai (knife-hand deflection) and by placing your left hand on his right arm, allow it to fall only through the weight of your own arm. As it drops, turn his wrist palm up and grasp the back of his right hand by controlling with the small finger side of your left hand. Then, throw the opponent down by controlling his right arm in this manner. After throwing him, keep his right elbow on the floor, and position his right wrist to face his legs by clenching the meridian of the large intestine. Through this action, the opponent loses freedom of movement throughout his entire body.

Chapter 15
Never do it too much

Chapter 16

"Front"

◈ Should not use the half-open posture

Unless one has a rather deep knowledge of Hakkoryu, they might consider that Hakkoryu should be categorised in the same group as Daito-ryu and Aikido. This is, in one sense, correct, but there is one major difference between them that is not well known. In Hakkoryu, they do not utilize the half-open posture (Hanmi).

It is their very basic concept to utilize a front-facing posture, and accordingly, based on that concept, if one attempts to use a half-open stance, it means that he will lose his balance.

Of course, using the half-open stance has merit in reducing the target area of the body susceptible to attack.

I asked Okuyama 2nd Soke about that point—for instance, if the opponent attacks with a straight punch.

Then Okuyama 2nd Soke showed me Shuto Barai (sweeping block) as shown in [photos 16-1].

"If the attack is higher than your chest, raise your Shuto to block upwards and if it is lower, drop it down to block with your Shuto downwards. It is easy, isn't it? This is because they are basically the same motion, only moving in different directions."

Yes, it might be easy, but in fact, it is not so easy in practice—so I was thinking upon hearing his explanation. Then, Okuyama 2nd Soke probably noticed what I was thinking and added the following very important explanation.

"It is important that you relax and not put any force into your arm. By putting less force in your arm, it can move faster. You should leverage the

Chapter 16
"Front"

If the punch is higher than chest height, then block it by raising up your hand (photo above), if lower, then drop it down (photo below). This motion is so simple that one can perform this block immediately. If you relax your arm and just try to use its weight, you can block the punch unexpectedly easier. It is important to abandon force in your arm and you should not attempt to avoid the punch, but keep the centre of your body still. As long as you maintain proper posturing, you can relax yourself.

photos 16-1

arms' weight, but not use force."

Then Okuyama 2nd Soke dropped his Shuto against my wrist and I immediately received a sharp pain that surprised me. He applied only the "arm's weight", but this created such great kinetic energy that it was really surprising. In the first place, Okuyama 2nd Soke has heavy arms, and if he holds out his arm to the front as shown in [photos 16-1], you get a feeling that you can never launch an attack against him.

That feeling comes from your perception of his arm as a huge obstructive object.

"In case of emergency, it is important that you can abandon force from your arm. If you try to make a half-open stance, or try to escape from the attack, it does not work. This is because as soon as you attempt those actions you put force in your arm."

Well, that is why it is important to assume a front facing posture without escaping from the attack, which is the basic concept of Hakkoryu.

However there are some motions to avert the attack by using the half-open posture in Hakkoryu. And, for Daito-ryu and Aikido, where they preserve techniques for defence against an attack using a Katana (sword), the half-open posture is effective in not exposing the weak point of Seichusen (centre line of the body) to attack by the opponent.

In fact, they have techniques against a sword attack in Hakkoryu. This made me wonder how they handle the Katana in such techniques.

Okuyama 2nd Soke showed me the following two examples, [photos 16-2]. Each technique consists of complicated sequences, but here, he showed only the beginning stage where the opponent attacks with the Katana.

As I already expected, Okuyama 2nd Soke handled the Katana attack from front regardless of which direction the attack comes, from the side or from above. In fact, the Katana is a strong weapon, but the way of attack is restricted. If you step forward to come closer to the attacker, this is likely the safest direction, rather than trying to escape to the outside.

"You should not try to escape from the attack. If you do so, you unbalance yourself. You should step forward against the attack with a relaxed mind."

In reality, if you are faced with an attacker wielding a Katana, you would become extremely fearful in anticipation of being cut and how you might escape the attack….. Such thinking makes you completely tense. Here, the important point is not how you can step in with the best timing, but how you can step in without hesitation. That is important.

"After all, to assume the half-open posture is a matter of probability. It can work against the attack from above, but will not work for the side attack. Then, you have to precisely anticipate how the opponent shall attack you. Of course it is important to react to the attack prop-

Chapter 16
"Front"

Step forward to the front even against a sword attack   photos 16-2

Shown here are two attacks from different cutting directions. Okuyama 2nd Soke blocks the attack by stepping directly forward. It looks like he uses perfect timing, but the most important point should be to step forward without hesitation. The opponent who starts to cut has already started unbalancing himself through his own action. Consequently, if you can prevent yourself from becoming unbalanced, you can easily block the opponent's cutting action.

For a side cut

For a downward cut

163

erly in Bujutsu, but if you start trying to anticipate the exact way the opponent may attack you, it is no use."

Fear and thought might cause that anticipation. Before the actual attack begins, you start fearing and anticipating the way of attack to plan for how to escape from it. To assume a front posture lets you give up that fear and anticipation. You do not have to think over from where the attack may come, right or left. You just maintain the front facing posture, which is the strongest stance against the attacker in front of you.

◈ Give your weapon away to the opponent

Everybody has their own weak points, like stronger opponents, things they are not skilled at, fear of certain objects (animals, insects, etc.), or situations, such as a fear of heights. And if one has no choice but to face such situations that they lack skill in, or are fearful of, what should or could they do? I speculate that in most cases, they cannot face these things directly, such as things they fear, and therefore cannot face such things directly to the front, head-on. Because of this fear, they assume a half-open posture, just to prepare their escape (from an opponent, for instance). As a result they become weak, both mentally and physically. And in such situations, they cannot function properly.

It does not matter whether your opponent is stronger or weaker than yourself; you have to face your opponent directly to the front if you really want to defeat them. This applies to anything, including people, or difficult situations.

When I was associating such things, Okuyama 2nd Soke took up a stick. This time Okuyama 2nd Soke wields a weapon, but the opponent is unarmed. Then the opponent grasps the stick to try to take it away from Okuyama 2nd Soke.

"In this case you have a mental blockage that is different than the previous case. You feel a sense of superiority because you have a weapon, while the opponent does not. And, if he could take your weapon away, the position would be drastically reversed. So, you develop the intention that your weapon will never be taken away from you and you attempt to pull the stick back using power. That is very bad. If you are cool-headed, you would probably

Chapter 16
"Front"

try to swing the stick to the left and right, or try to make some kind of trick motion to prevent the stick from being taken away. But the correct answer for this case is the same as before, just to step forward,"

Okuyama 2nd Soke did not resist the opponent's pulling motion but simply stepped forward to the front, which resulted in the opponent becoming unbalanced.

"Never fixate on your weapon. Just let him take hold of it. If you can calm yourself with such a way of thinking, you can take the initiative in this situation."

This is the practise of Hakkoryu's important concept of "no resistance". You can carry out this concept with your own intention, not by the opponent's intention, because you move forward without escaping.

In Hakkoryu they say that one square meter of space is enough to apply techniques. They really do not move much during the execution of techniques.

"If you move around you unbalance yourself. You do not need to move to the left or right. Just keep your front posture and remain in-balance. That is Hakkoryu's technique. I can also say that if you can maintain your own balance, the opponent himself becomes unbalanced as a consequence."

The result of this mental effect could be immense because you do not need to do anything but simply try to keep your front posture and maintain your own balance. Then you have no straining or tenseness in your body and you can perform to the best of your ability as a result.

If it is possible, I wish I could practice this in my everyday life. You do not need to injure others, even for self-defence. It is important how you maintain yourself, and never try to escape from any difficulties.

In fact, there is no other solution to overcome your weaknesses than to just face them directly.

I am now convinced that I will deal with difficult matters face-to-face, directly to the front. If I will succeed in overcoming them in such a way, I will become free from any mental impasse and make the best of my ability.

Tsue Osae Dori photos 16-3
(Walking Stick Art, Kaiden/Okuden level)

The opponent grasps your stick. Your strong advantage of using the weapon will drastically change if the stick is taken away by the opponent. But, do not worry about this and do not pull back on the stick to prevent it being taken away. You just step directly forward while grasping the stick between the opponent's hands. While continuing to face the opponent and continuing to step directly forward, he will lose his balance completely. Then apply Gakun to his left wrist with your right hand and control him. Take him down to the floor on his stomach after placing the stick through his left armpit and between his legs. Finally, control the end of the stick using your right foot. Now pinned, the opponent cannot move at all.

Chapter 16
"Front"

Chapter 17

Where am I?

◉ The techniques become effective by utilising gravity

In the previous chapter, I related that Hakkoryu techniques can work in such a small space as only one square meter. This means that in Hakkoryu they do not move around, and they also do not need to perform retreating or follow through motions.

"In case you have to fight against a Karate-ka, you had better take him into a toilet stall and fight there," said Okuyama 2nd Soke, half-jokingly. In fact, they can even fight in such a small space as a toilet stall. That is Hakkoryu. Are there any other Bujutsu like that?

Not only for kicking and punching techniques, but also for Taijutsu systems (body arts), you need some horizontal space to fight. For instance, to swing the opponent left and right to unbalance him, and to use his rushing inertia to execute techniques.

Then I asked Okuyama 2nd Soke how they can apply their techniques in such a confined space.

"We use vertical force, or gravity."

It is easy to just say use gravity, but this is very difficult to put into practice—at least as far as I understood. This might be because most of us today classify our motion as moving against the force of gravity. Many of the readers may not think this way, but I must confess, this was my own belief. If we are free from the constraints of gravity, we could move much faster and could lift much heavier mass. We surely dream of how it would be easy in the world if we could live without gravity. Consequently, we do not even entertain the idea of how to leverage gravity.

Anyway, let's observe this in an actual technique. The photos [photos

Chapter 17
Where am I?

17-1] show Uchikomi Dori (Strike Inside Art, 2nd Dan level). As a consequence, it is similar to many common techniques found in the other styles of Jujutsu. But, in the case of Hakkoryu, the control is done without using horizontal unbalancing motion. It is excellent!

I asked Okuyama 2nd Soke to demonstrate one more time. Because techniques end so quickly in Hakkoryu, I do not have enough time to analyse them by only watching once. This request of demonstrating the technique one more time has become common during this interview. Mr. Okawa, who takes on the role of Uke (attacker), tries to appeal to me with his eyes not to ask this so often because every time I ask, he receives such sharp pain over and over again from Okuyama 2nd Soke. This time, he also tried to appeal to me, but I just ignored it.

Okawa Shihan tried to throw a punch at Okuyama 2nd Soke's face, and Okuyama 2nd Soke received it with excellent timing, without flailing at it or trying to grasp at it.

"You should not resist against the attacker's punch," said Okuyama 2nd Soke.

'No resistance' is a basic principle of Hakkoryu, and you do not have to put force into your blocking hands or arms.

Okuyama 2nd Soke guided Okawa Shihan's right hand so that its small finger side faced upward and he immediately pinned him down as before.

"Here again, you do not pin him downward using power. You just hang from his wrist."

"Hang from his wrist?"

Such wording is never used in the technical explanations of Bujutsu. If you explain that you transfer your weight to the opponent's wrist, then I could understand what that means. But "hang from the wrist", what does that mean?

Okuyama 2nd Soke explained, "In this case you tend to twist on the opponent's wrist, but it does not work. If you intend to apply a technique, it does not work. You should not use power, but harness the arm's weight by abandoning your power. That is why I say "hang from the wrist"."

That makes sense. Everybody certainly anticipates putting power in the arms to move them downwards. In other words, it is the same motion as raising your body by pushing your arms downwards. You put your hand on the

Uchikomi Dori   photos 17-1
(Strike Inside Art, 2nd Dan level)

Okawa Shihan tried to throw a punch at Okuyama 2nd Soke's face, and Okuyama 2nd Soke received it without flailing or grasping at it, but just by applying his hands to his arm.

Okuyama 2nd Soke guided Okawa Shihan's right hand so that its small finger side faced upward, and he immediately pinned him downward.

In other Jujutsu Ryuha (schools), they have Kuden (oral teachings) for this technique, such as making the opponent's arm form an "S" shape in the horizontal plane, or to hold the opponent's hand against one's chest to make the control surer. But in Hakkoryu they do not have such Kuden. Although they explain how to lock the opponent's wrist, the image of this motion is to drop down on the opponent's body all at once.

table and push on it when you want to raise your body up. Thus, by using this motion, you do not just drop the opponent's wrist, you use the same motion as when trying to push yourself up.

It has long since passed many years ago in several fields of study that it was advised to relax yourself through the abandonment of physical strength or power. But the fact remains that this is not only quite difficult to practice, but also to teach. Because people tend to create tension unconsciously, you

Chapter 17
Where am I?

have to teach them not to do so unconsciously. Hakkoryu has several excellent ways of explaining how to do it. This "hang from the wrist" is one example of such a clever explanation. If you consider the meaning deeply, you should be able to grasp it.

In reality, you could never hang your weight from his wrist in the same way you would hang yourself from a branch of a tree. But at the moment you succeed in relaxing yourself as if to hang from his wrist, the weight of both of your arms' will be applied to the opponent's wrist. That weight creates an unexpectedly large force onto the wrist.

By the way, one arm has 4-5 kg of mass (8-11 lbs), so both arms total 10 kg of mass (22 lbs). Just imagine that 10 kg of mass will be put on the end of an arm you stretch out horizontally. You could never support such a heavy object with just your one arm.

Moreover, the words "hang from" coveys a special Hakkoryu concept, i.e., not to resist but go along with the opponent in a natural motion. You do not control the other person from a higher position, but from the same height, or even from a lower height position from where you maintain control of the other person. That is the meaning of "hang from".

Also, the motion is not active at all. It all depends on the other person. If you can make your mental state "hang from" in a crisis situation, you can surely relax yourself.

◉ Apply the technique from a distance

The photos [photos 17-2] show Mune Osae Dori (Chest Pin Art, Kaiden level). At a glance, its ending looks quite similar to the former technique, Uchikomi Dori. However, if you watch it in detail, the opponent's hand is not turned all the way over so the small finger side is up. As such, it should essentially be a different technique. But they still look quite similar to each other. This is probably because both techniques leverage the force created by gravity to unbalance the opponent.

This technique works immediately, at the moment the opponent begins attacking. The Tori (defender) seems to do nothing and at the instant of Uke's (attacker) attack, controls Uke. So, it is done quite fast.

Regarding this technique, Okuyama 2nd Soke was once told by the

Chapter 17
Where am I?

founder (1st Soke) that he should imagine at that moment he had been by their neighbour's house, and he should have applied the technique from there.

"Do you understand the meaning?" Okuyama 2nd Soke asked me.

"What does it mean?"

"It means you should not be here to fight against your opponent. You should watch the situation from a distance so that you can have an overview."

With this explanation, I understood that mentally, you put yourself several meters away so that you can have a clear overview of the situation. But I soon discovered that I had the wrong interpretation. It is important that you should place yourself far enough away to create a non-fighting relationship with your opponent. In such a distant place where you do not need to fight, or cannot physically fight, you can eliminate your intention to react to the opponent's attack, reverse his hand by which he grasped your body, or how to twist it. First and foremost, you can eliminate your fear of being attacked because of the vast distance. This is an enormous metal effect.

The founder (1st Soke) also told his students to apply techniques as if they were located at Omiya train station, which is located 20 minutes away from here by foot. If the instruction is to be so far away, we might become lost and not know what direction we face, or not be able to see what is happening, etc. Then, I suddenly noticed that I should not try to see the situation. You should leave behind what you see subjectively.

In case you see the situation as subjective, and from a confrontational relationship, you tend to become stuck in such a way of thinking. Then you are forced to do something to escape or overcome the situation. Thus, you become anxious, either consciously or unconsciously.

The biggest obstacle that blocks development in Bujutsu is an unconscious tension. This is created unconsciously, so it is very difficult to change it. Hakkoryu gives you important hints on how to become free from such unconscious tension.

In most cases in Bujutsu, what you can see with your eyes as an object is your enemy. Accordingly, in most Bujutsu, a lot of themes have been studied regarding how you should react against the enemy.

But in Hakkoryu, the theme is how you are, not how to react against your enemy. They do not explain how the mental state should be, but focus on a more fundamental matter—how you should be. They require you to forget yourself and see the 'whole' in a very real sense. If one can realize this teaching, one could probably attain real strength. In that sense, the great masters of old all left similar teachings or sayings.

"Seeing with the eyes is weak; but seeing with the heart is strong."

On my return to Omiya station, where I had already passed by several times, for the first time I noticed an attractive shop. Then, feeling the warm weather of early spring, I began feeling that perhaps I could abandon power after all.

Mune Osae Dori photos 17-2
(Chest Pin Art, Kaiden level)

This technique works immediately at the moment the opponents starts grasping the Tori's Joi (jacket) around the chest.

We do not see any initial physical motion or

Chapter 17
Where am I?

set-up, such as holding the opponent's hand against the chest, or turning it over. Avoiding any conflict or tension against the opponent's grasping power on your chest you apply the force of gravity through the opponent to drop him down. The technique consists of such a simple motion, but that is why it is so powerful.

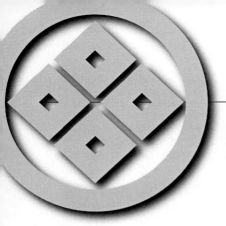

Chapter 18

San Dai Kichu (Three Great Pillars)

◈ Three essential points

This is the last chapter and I definitely want to introduce one particular theme in this book, the three great pillars. This is the highest level of Hakkoryu that is difficult to learn, because it is the ultimate secret of the art. Consequently, I would like to know more about what this level contains.

Okuyama 2nd Soke explained, "Frankly speaking, the concept of the three great pillars did not exist in the early days of Hakkoryu. It was developed by the founder (1st Soke) in 1974. There was a training camp called Yotsume Ryo at Kujukuri in Chiba prefecture, which we do not have anymore. The concepts were taught for the first time by the founder at this training camp. The camp was located near the beach and around twenty people were training on the beach every day. At that time the founder started teaching the participants these concepts in a very intensive way.

What specifically did the founder teach his students at that time? The three great pillars are not techniques. They consist of Roken Senretsu (Shoulder of the Road), Kengai Kenshin (Standing at the Edge of the Cliff) and Shinki Yakujou (God Skin)—but again, these are not techniques. In Hakkoryu, every student begins learning the system starting with the techniques of 1st Dan, then 2nd Dan, 3rd Dan, 4th Dan, and beyond that, the Shihan techniques, followed by the techniques of Kaiden. At the final stage they learn these three great pillars. Regardless, when one reaches the Shihan level, he/she has the right to start his/her own Dojo and teach their own students. At that level they know all the techniques, but they should start doubting if they have truly mastered all these techniques. That is the Shihan level. Then they learn these three great pillars, which finally gives them

Chapter 18
San Dai Kichu (Three Great Pillars)

confidence. These three great pillars are the key, so to speak, that unlocks all the final secrets in each of the techniques."

Well then, it might be more like a refinement of all the techniques.

In the case that it was just some specific technical knowledge relating to physical motion, then it could certainly be taught at the beginning stages, but this is not the case. One must build up experience with enough training, and only at the level where one has mastered techniques well enough than he/she could finally understand what these concepts are.

In many Bujutsu, we often hear that the very first techniques one learns at the beginning are often the ultimate, highest level techniques. However, this does not mean that one can reach the highest level after he/she has only mastered the initial fundamental techniques.

Okuyama 2nd Soke showed me the difference between knowing and not knowing these concepts by using the technique of Hakko Dori as an example, although he mentioned that the difference might not be apparent in the photos.

Hakko Dori seems like a technique for releasing your grasped wrists, first by raising one arm, then the other, but its purpose is just to raise your grasped arm.

"It is difficult to just raise your grasped arm. If you use power, you cannot do it."

Then please remember the advice given earlier of trying to scratch your ear that itches, which was explained in Chapter 1. This contains the knowledge of how to raise your arm (refer to [photos 18-1], the fist part).

"Now I will show you Hakko Dori after knowing the concept of Roken Senretsu." Well, I wonder if the readers can recognise the difference, as shown in [photos 18-1], the latter part.

First, you probably noticed that by the 3rd photo, the opponent was already unbalanced much more, but this is not because of Roken Senretsu. In the basic Hakko Dori, if the opponent tries to bear down with their weight, trying not to become unbalanced, it results in them becoming even more unbalanced. This is the case shown in the 3rd photo.

Then what is the difference?

As Okuyama 2nd Soke explained, it is indeed quite difficult to recognise

177

Hakko Dori   photos 18-1
(1st Dan level)

Okuyama 2nd Soke raises his grasped wrists one after the other. If you put force in your arms, you cannot raise them. There is a Kuden that you should raise your hand as if to scratch your itchy ear. It is not the purpose to unbalance the opponent in this technique, so when the opponent cannot continue to maintain their hold on your wrist, you release it from their grasp. As a result, it looks like a simple wrist escape technique. In the next photo sequence, Okuyama 2nd Soke applied the concepts contained within the three great pillars, and the opponent's shoulder had already begun to tense-up when he grasped Okuyama 2nd Soke's wrists. He had already started to become unstable, even at that beginning stage.

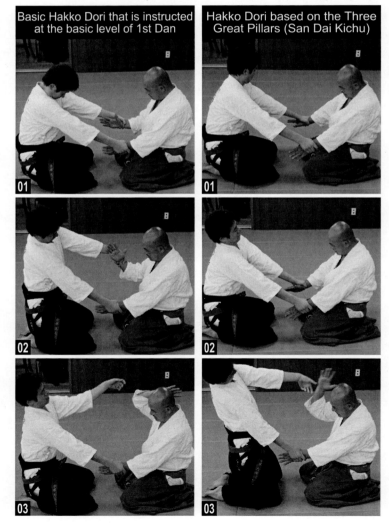

Chapter 18
San Dai Kichu (Three Great Pillars)

the difference only by looking at the photos. But if you can observe the difference closely with your eyes, you are sure to spot the very subtle difference.

For the version of Hakko Dori based on the three great pillars, the opponent showed some signs that he was being controlled before Okuyama 2nd Soke raised his hand. This means that the opponent was already beginning to become unstable, even before Okuyama 2nd Soke started raising his hand.

In Hakkoryu they have a written explanation regarding these three great pillars and each of the concepts is described in detail. After receiving special permission from Okuyama 2nd Soke, I was able to read these written explanations. That said, for an outsider like me, it was rather difficult to understand the content. The explanations contain expressive terminology that only a person who has sufficiently deep knowledge of Hakkoryu could understand.

First of all, let's define what "Roken" means.

"It sounds like an abstract expression that affects all the techniques, but its meaning is quite concrete. Here, Roken means the route, or road, taken by the meridians (keiraku) to reach the shoulder of the human body. Of course it has deeper meaning, though."

This explanation made my understanding a little clearer. In most situations and martial arts, the opponent begins their attack by grasping or hitting with their hands. This is also the case in Hakkoryu. Then when you touch the opponent's hand as he attacks you, you immediately lock-up (Kime) his shoulder via that meridian route from hand to shoulder. In this case, Kime does not mean a physical joint lock. It relates to a gentler, but even stronger control of the opponent that can be clearly felt but not easily seen.

I wanted to understand this better, but it is a secret part of the curriculum and normally would not even be shown to outsiders. Even if it was explained orally, an outsider might never understand what it truly is. Then, Okuyama 2nd Soke added the following explanation which aided my understanding.

"The secret exists in how you can make invisible (i.e., not physical) Kime to the opponent's hand."

◉ Invisible Unbalancing

Although I still could not understand what Roken Senretsu was very well, Okuyama 2nd Soke showed me several techniques based on the teaching of Roken Senretsu. In fact, he utilized Roken Senretsu for all the techniques he had demonstrated thus far. After hearing his explanation, the techniques being demonstrated (which I had already seen several times at this point), now look surprisingly different to me.

On [photos 18-2], Konoha Gaeshi (Leaf Reversal, 2nd Dan technique) is shown. The opponent first grasps your sleeve then tries to strike you. You block his strike and grasp the back of his fist to execute this technique. Okuyama 2nd Soke demonstrated this technique quite effortlessly, but in actuality, the action he showed would be rather difficult to perform. If Okuyama 2nd Soke did not execute Kime when he touched the opponent's fist, he could not grasp the back of his hand as easily. So, for this action, Roken Senretsu should have been applied.

Besides the unbalancing by dropping down the wrist and arm shown in [photos 18-2], no.4 and 5, as well as the final takedown and pin shown in no.6, the importance of bending the opponent's wrist is just a method to guide the opponent. Okuyama 2nd Soke never bent the opponent's wrist using power to generate pain. It is only because Okuyama 2nd Soke uses invisible Kime that he can perform these actions so smoothly.

The three great pillars are not secret techniques that can be added to the other techniques. It may even be the case that somebody, without knowing it, has already stated mastering these from the very beginning. It is such primitive and subtle knowledge. When one has mastered a great number of techniques and is used to applying those techniques, then he tends to stick to the form too much. The concepts of the three great pillars remind the person who has fallen into such a situation the correct way. By realizing these concepts, one's techniques might change completely. Every form of Bujutsu may have their own method for teaching such secret knowledge, but you cannot discover or notice it easily. In Hakkoryu, they discovered this secret knowledge and systematized it so that their students could learn it. Their highly refined teaching system is really surprising.

Chapter 18
San Dai Kichu (Three Great Pillars)

Here, I have to apologize to the readers that I could only introduce one of the three great pillars, Roken Senretsu. However, these concepts are the ultimate highest level teachings of Hakkoryu, so Okuyama 2nd Soke introducing even one of them is already a special and exceptional case. I want to thank Okuyama 2nd Soke so much for showing many of the deepest and most secret teachings of Hakkoryu. I cannot find proper words by which I can express my deep appreciation to Okuyama 2nd Soke. It is so generous of Okuyama 2nd Soke to show and explain so many secrets, but of course, he knows that one can never truly understand or master such things by only hearing about them, or by reading their explanations. Like the three great pillars, knowledge that cannot be seen is the most important knowledge.

More than anything, his generous personality, by which he showed so many important things without closing in the veil of secrecy, personifies the Hakkoryu concepts of "no challenge, no resistance, and no injury".

Every time I met with Okuyama 2nd Soke and his students for my interview, I felt as though I received some form of unseen energy from them. That is my frank impression at the end of this book. It might also be a lingering mental effect of some kind. Again, it is surprising that a Bujutsu has such miraculous power.

Konoha Gaeshi photos 18-2
(2nd Dan level)

The opponent grasped the sleeve of Okuyama 2nd Soke and attempted to strike with the other hand. Okuyama 2nd Soke blocked his strike, then secured his fist/wrist to take the opponent down. After dropping him down to the floor, he controlled the opponent using a one-handed grip on his wrist to prevent him from getting back up. There is another version of the technique in which you secure the opponent's hand before he makes a fist and starts his strike. In this case, it is easier to hold his hand. But in this version of the technique, it is quite difficult to shift from the blocking motion to securing the opponent's fist. During the stage of the technique shown in photo 2, you should apply invisible Kime to the opponent at the moment your hand contacted his wrist. In the throwing motion shown in photos 5 and 6, Okuyama 2nd Soke never uses pain to control the opponent. Here he uses Roken Senretsu.

Chapter 18
San Dai Kichu (Three Great Pillars)

Supplement

How to defend yourself using a one finger strike

◈ Hakkoryu's essence condensed into 18 articles

Originally, Hakkoryu was specialised in Goshinjutsu (self-defence techniques), and they have something called the "18 Goshin Articles". This is namely 18 self-defence techniques classified by various ways of attack.

The "18 Goshin Articles" was created by the founder (1st Soke) during the Second World War (WWII). He aimed to provide hand-to-hand combat instruction for the Japanese people who were ready to fight against the U.S. Army during the expected invasion of Japan.

"That is why the original version contained a lot of dangerous killing techniques. Then, after the war, the founder revised these "18 Goshin Articles" by eliminating the dangerous parts."

Here, it is important to mention that the "18 Goshin Articles" were not created for students of Hakkoryu. It was created for all citizens, so that they

They issued these 18 Goshin Articles as a booklet with the title of "Hakkoryu Gakai Hen". This was issued by the Hakkoryu Headquarters (Honbu). The book shown in this photo was issued in 2001. The first edition was issued in 1950.

Supplement
How to defend yourself using a one finger strike

The founder, Okuyama 1st Soke (seen in the back right of the photo) teaches his Goshinjutsu system to students of a girls school.

This photo was taken at the lecture entitled "Goshin", which was held at Kokura-City in Kyushu.

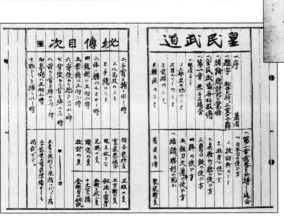

This booklet is the origin of the 18 Goshin Articles, which was issued in 1945 and entitled "Komin Budo Hiden" (Secret Essence of Budo for Japanese Citizens). It intended to demonstrate how to fight against the enemy using hand-to-hand combat, so it describes a lot of killing techniques.

could protect themselves without basic knowledge or experience in the Hakkoryu system itself, which takes several levels of instruction to master.

Is it really possible that one can learn the essence of Hakkoryu in such a short period of time?

"Yes, it is possible up to a certain level. It is not difficult to learn Hakkoryu in the first place. In Hakkoryu, people attempt to master what is not easily mastered, although this should not be difficult. Such teachings are cleverly arranged in these "18 Goshin Articles."

◈ No challenge, no resistance and no injury

The contents of the "18 Goshin Articles" are shown in [table 19-1]. There are 18 techniques for 10 different situations.

Let's read the first article.

"In the standing posture, an enemy grasps both of my wrists and tries to attack me. I immediately abandon power from my arms and shoulders so that both hands hang from the shoulders naturally. Without making fists, I slap the enemy's eyes using my fingertips. When you use the fingers of the right hand, you step forward the same side (right) foot. This is the same basic motion of traditional Japanese dance. In some other forms of Bujutsu, they step forward with the opposite side foot of the hand that attacks. This is an unscientific action that is not based on the concept of relative physics. The left hand should always be moved with the left foot. In this situation, the enemy senses the danger to his face and releases his grasp by stepping back. It does not matter how strongly he grasped your wrists. Then, I strike his solar plexus lightly with the tip of my thumb. It is important not to make a fist to avoid putting force into it, and rush forward into him using the body. No matter how big a guy the enemy is, you can control him through this action."

Here, it does not say anything about what you should do against the enemy's attacking hand. Abandoning your power is the most important thing you should do. If you try to use power, you will immediately realise that it is no use to compete with the enemy by power. If he is stronger than you, he will pull you very easily. If you try to compete with him using power, there is not much chance you will succeed in your defence.

Supplement

How to defend yourself using a one finger strike

18 Goshin Articles

1. In the case your wrist(s) is grasped
   The 1st - the 3rd article
2. In the case the attacker tries to grab you
   The 4th - the 5th article
3. In the case you are hugged from behind
   The 6th article
4. In the case your neck is choked
   The 7th - the 9th article
5. In the case the clothing around your chest is grasped
   The 10th - the 11th article
6. In the case the attacker tries to punch you
   The 12th - the 13th article
7. In case you arrest the attacker
   The 14th article
8. In the case your bag is taken away
   The 15th article
9. In the case the attacker has a weapon
   The 16th - the 17th article
10. In the case you are surrounded by multiple attackers
    The 18th article

table 19-1

It becomes possible to move freely by your own intent if you do not resist with power and avoid becoming tense. "No challenge, no resistance and no injury" are the three great principles in Hakkoryu.

For this 1st article, the movement itself is arranged in such a manner (refer to [photos 19-1]). You just react to the enemy's pulling motion by pushing your body forward—there is no conflict.

You attack the enemy's eye with you fingertip. But the real purpose is not to gouge his eyes out, but to let him falter and release his grip, or lose his balance. If you are successful in unbalancing him, strike his solar plexus (Atemi) to create an opening to escape from his attack.

The 1st article   photos 19-1

In case the attacker grasps both of your wrists, you try to hang both grasped arms down by relaxing them and choose one of your hands whose fingertips you direct toward the opponent's eyes. At the same time, you rush in toward him with the same side foot stepping forward. When the attacker releases his grasp, or he loses balance, you execute a strike (Atemi) to his solar plexus with the opposite hand while stepping forward with the same side foot.

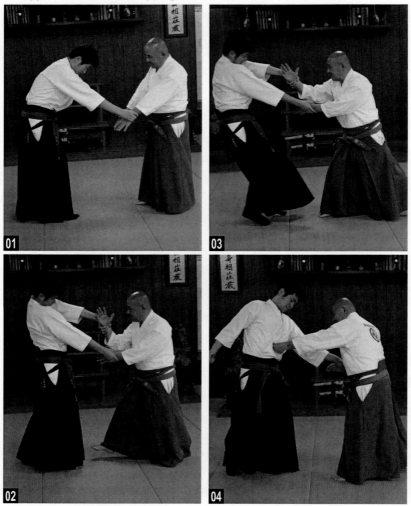

Supplement
How to defend yourself using a one finger strike

POINT

Do not use force and relax yourself.

It is the major principle of Hakkoryu not to use force, but to relax yourself. This is important for achieving the following two points:
1) You do not let the attacker move you as he intends (i.e., not to be pulled).
2) You move as you will (i.e., you rush toward the attacker with the fingertips of one hand aiming toward his eyes).

You should try those actions without tensing up as much as possible. It is important knowing at this stage that you can realize these movements only by avoiding tension.

If you watch the 1st article carefully, the movements of both parties are done in the same direction, which does not clash but harmonizes. You do not need to generate power which exceeds the other's power at all.

Use the same side arm and foot while moving

This is the "same side theory" which recognises the idea of "conformity of the whole body". This theory is symbolized by Namba and proves its rationality in many Koryu Kenjutsu and Jujutsu schools. In Hakkoryu, they also place importance on this same side theory, which helps to eliminate unnecessary force. We can better understand their use of this because they refer to traditional Japanese dance, which utilizes this same side motion. If one steps forward with their right foot while also swinging the left arm forward, this results in the twisting of the upper body. Through this way of moving, one tends to move only the upper body or arms. This causes one to use force in the arms. In this process, you need to move forward quickly without putting force in the arms.

POINT

189

The Atemi used here is not a simple Atemi, which is often used in Jujutsu.

◈ Ate (hit) using only one finger

In [photos 19-2], the 5th article is shown. This is applied at the moment the enemy touches you, therefore, it is applicable for a striking attack.

The action is very simple. Just perform a strike (Ate) to his armpit.

"For most of the attacking postures, Ate (a strike or hit) with one finger might be effective. In the case you are attacked, if you hit or kick him back using power, it simply applies damage to him and such action cannot be considered real Goshin technique, which should not injure the attacker unnecessarily. When the enemy attacks you with violence, you can make a light Ate to stimulate his sensory nerves, which uses a slow in push and fast out pulling method of delivery. In fact, this is the most important point for Goshin arts in the modern era. In this way you can neutralise the enemy's violence and control him effortlessly."

The strike is not made using your fist, or base of the palm, but with the tip of the thumb. Everyone may doubt that you can execute a strong strike in this way, but you actually do not hit strongly.

The hand shape for this strike is shown in [photos 19-2], "Ate should be made using the tip of the thumb".

"In Hakkoryu we do not perform strikes to destroy the enemy's body, but to apply pain and weaken him. So you just stimulate a small point. Or, I should say that it is much better to stimulate him through a small point. As the founder described, the strike should be made just to stimulate the enemy's sensory nerves. For that purpose the action is quicker pulling back after contact is made than striking forward. It is the same as the concept used in Koho Shiatsu.

Koho Shiatsu, as has already been described several times, is a healing method in Hakkoryu in which one stimulates the meridians using finger pressure to improve the function of the internal organs. It actually delivers sharp and strong pain in the same way as Jujutsu's Ate. It is just for an instant, but one receives a sharp pain as if lightning flows through the inside of your body when your sensory nerves are stimulated. It is really surprising how such a strong amount of pain can be created using this method of Shiatsu.

Supplement
How to defend yourself using a one finger strike

The 5th article   photos 19-2

In the moment the attacker tried to make contact with you (in this case to strike), execute a strike (Ate) to his armpit while bending low from the knees. If you try to strike strongly, your speed is reduced. You only need to "strike" using the tip of the thumb (refer to the photo "Ate should be made using the tip of the thumb"). If you try to use force during your strike, you become tense, and it goes without saying that this is forbidden in Hakkoryu. The aim of this strike is not to destroy the attacker's body but to apply pain, so the tip of the thumb is enough to execute the desired pin-point stimulation.

As one understands this theory deeper, they can eliminate even more unnecessary force and their strike will become even faster.

191

POINT

Ate should be made using the tip of the thumb

In Hakkoryu, the strike (Ate) should not be done using the fist, but the tip of the thumb as shown in the photo. You might be worried that you will injure your thumb because of its apparent weak design for striking, but the strike itself is only just a light touch, so there is no need to worry about injuring your thumb. If your aim is only to apply pain, this is more effective. You also do not need to push the tip of the thumb deeper into the opponent's body. It is more important how you pull back, or retract the strike.

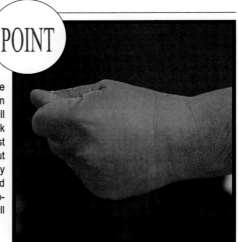

Ate is the same as Shiatsu

The knowledge of how to apply the strike effectively is the same as Koho Shiatsu. In the case of Koho Shiatsu, they have a three-step process, as shown in pictures. The 3rd step of releasing your finger is the most important step to make Shiatsu effective. This also applies to striking (Ate). It is less important how strongly you press with your finger during the 2nd step.

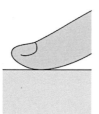

1 Touch

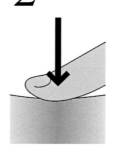

2 Press

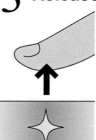

3 Release

Supplement
How to defend yourself using a one finger strike

The secret is likely in the push/pull method of delivery, rather than using no power.

"It is no use to attempt Koho Shiatsu using power. Although it just looks like pushing with the finger, it consists of the three steps of touch, press and release. You never apply power by pressing. The moment you release your finger is the most important point to stimulate the sensory nerves."

That is why the pain appears only for an instant. However, even though it is only for an instant, it causes enormous pain and works to stop the enemy's action. Because of this unexpectedly intense pain, he releases his grip involuntarily.

Let's imagine trying to make a counterstrike using a normal Atemi, which would be quite difficult. From the positioning you do not have enough space to gain sufficient momentum to apply an effective body blow. Such a blow to the body is only possible by professional boxers.

Besides, this thumb strike is surprisingly fast because it is just touching with the tip of the thumb. The movement is natural and quick. Starting the action itself is quick and the overall speed is very fast. Again, I realise the importance of being relaxed. Here, the mental effect which Hakkoryu places great importance on works very effectively. Because you do not need to release the enemy's grasp using power, there is no need to make a counter-strike with power. You can rest easy knowing that you can react against this attack with just one thumb. It does not matter how strong the attacker may be. This way of thinking makes you calm and results in the high speed of your strike (Ate).

There are probably many people who doubt this, and may wonder, "Does it really not matter how strong the enemy is?"

◈ It is better if the enemy uses more power for his attack

On [photos 19-3] we introduce the 3rd Goshin article.

In the same manner as the 1st Goshin article described previously, it explains how to react in the case your wrist is grasped. For this article you use one finger to control the enemy.

"In the standing posture, an enemy grasps my right wrist and tries to take me away in a violent manner. I immediately abandon power from my right arm and shoulder, then pull back my right fingers just slightly enough to resist his pulling force. Consequently, the enemy applies even more strength to pull me more forcefully. At the moment he puts full power into his arm, I push with my left thumb at the point on his pulling arm (left) where he applies his strength. It does not matter exactly where the point is, above or below the elbow. The enemy immediately receives a sharp pain at that point and releases his grasp with a surprise, as he did not expect such intense pain.

The important knowledge is how you press your thumb into the enemy's arm. You push with the center of the thumb to stimulate the point as if to make a light strike, or Atemi, against that point."

By the way, you do not feel significant pain at the point where you should push, whether above or below the elbow, if you try to push it yourself, even with strong force. However, if another person pushes this same point when you try to attack them by grasping their arm, you feel tremendous pain.

"This is because the point turns into a weak point when the attacker puts power there. You might feel some degree of pain against the same point in a relaxed situation, but if you put as much power as possible into your arm, you will feel intense pain there. Accordingly, it makes it easier for you to handle the enemy if he uses more power for his attack", Okuyama 2nd Soke explained.

I understood this concept very well. We do not fear an enemy who tries to attack us with strength or power. If we do not fear them, we can make ourselves relaxed. If we can make ourselves relaxed, we can move freely. This is the precise positive result caused by such a mental effect.

If we mention that "you can control the enemy only using one finger",

Supplement
How to defend yourself using a one finger strike

The 3rd article photos 19-3

In case the attacker grasps your right wrist, you abandon force in that arm and pull your fingertips lightly to the side of your body. The attacker immediately reacts by putting force into his grasping arm to resist your pulling motion. Then, you squeeze right above or just below his elbow using your free left hand fingers like a claw. You do this with the image of making a light strike with the fingertips. The more force he puts into his arm, the more tense he will become. The more tense he becomes, the more pain he will receive using this clawing style strike and he cannot continue to maintain his grasp.

The weak point appears where the opponent is tense.

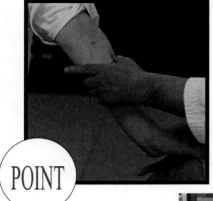

Considering the fact you create pain in the attacker by pressing and releasing your finger, you may believe that you have to press right on the exact spot of the weak point. But in Hakkoryu, the weak point is not as small as a pin-point (Note: This also applies to Koho Shiatsu. The place where they apply Shiatsu to cure illness is not a pin-point target, but the line of a meridian). The weak point is not always the place you feel pain when you are attacked. The place where you are tense becomes the weak point where you experience pain. In fact, if you are pressed by a single finger, you always receive intense pain everywhere you are pressed. It is really strange. (refer to the photo, no.2) Specifically, you will have a greater chance if someone attacks you with all of their power.

The editor tried to grasp Okuyama 2nd Soke's arm in any manner he wished, then Okuyama 2nd Soke squeezed his arm like a claw, which caused such enormous pain that the editor crouched down to escape from it.

The 9th article   photos 19-4

While you are lying on your back, the attacker assumes a mounted position and is attempting to choke you. This is normally a hopeless situation for you to find yourself, but if the opponent attacks you with such brute force, you have a very good chance of escape. You only need to push the tensed-up belly side of his belly using your thumbs and the opponent cannot continue their attack or maintain their posture due to the intense pain. In such a difficult situation, try to make yourself calm, because you know how to control the attacker using only one finger. Just relax yourself and start your counter-action to escape.

Supplement
How to defend yourself using a one finger strike

you surely assume that this would be a miracle technique that only a few masters could realise who have trained for many years. But in fact, 8 of the total 18 Goshin Articles, which could be grasped by everyone, are techniques executed using only one finger (including a strike using the thumb).

As Hakkoryu techniques go, there are plenty of variations with much higher level application. By the time one reaches the highest level of Hakkoryu, one can control the enemy using only a single finger. But, what the founder intended to show through the 18 Goshin Articles are techniques that can be applied by everyone. As Okuyama 2nd Soke mentioned previously, these are techniques that are actually not too difficult to learn, but still cannot be performed easily. I think this should be the most important point in Bujutsu and in Goshinjutsu.

To be relaxed so that one can move freely in a crisis situation. If one can accomplish this one simple thing, they can surely do what needs to be done in an emergency. "Only with a finger and not a fist" relays this message to us, I think.

Okuyama 2nd Soke concluded as follows.

"I often think that there is no value in a person looking strong. In an actual emergency situation, when one should protect himself, it might result in receiving serious damage from an opponent if one looks too "strong". You do not have to challenge or resist, and you do not need to seriously injure the opponent. At the moment one can find the action that is most vital to deal with the situation, one can abandon all that is unnecessary. At that moment, one can become a "strong" person in the true meaning of the word."

Conclusion

By Hakkoryu 2nd Soke, Okuyama Ryuho

In Hakkoryu we teach you to abandon force from your shoulders and arms in any situation. In fact, if you do not release this force you cannot leverage the power of your abdomen, and accordingly, you cannot triumph against violence. The abdomen is the place where our vigour exists, and is also the centre of our vitality, spirit, and the most important secret of all teachings emanates from this place.

There is only one system through which you can train this abdominal power. That is not through medicine, nor by fitness equipment, or by Zazen, but only by training in our Hakkoryu as the essence of Japanese Bugei (martial arts). Accordingly, training in Hakkoryu can be useful in the prevention of all kinds of illness.

It is often said that aging starts in the joints. So, it is useful to cure the deterioration of the joints and perform stretching exercises for all muscles of the body through physical movement. You can heal high blood pressure and gastrointestinal problems immediately.

And, the instant pain caused through each Hakkoryu technique stimulates all internal organs, and gives them vitality. Subsequently, it improves your overall health condition. Also, it might lead to a longer life, and the curing of all kind of neurosis.

People become more polite by learning Hakkoryu, and it brings prosperity in life, in addition to improving their physical condition which leads to a healthy and happy life for everyone.

●Supervisor
Hakkoryu 2nd Soke Okuyama Ryuho
Okuyama Ryuho, 2nd Soke of Hakkoryu was born in 1948. He began learning Koho Shiatsu at the age of 5 from his father, Okuyama Ryuho 1st Soke, founder of Hakkoryu Jujutsu. He succeeded the founder as 2nd Soke on April 1986. Since that time he has been busy teaching his many students, who have not only spread Hakkoryu throughout Japan, but also in over eight foreign countries.

●Editor
Monthly HIDEN editorial department

●Translator
Kurabe Makoto Shiseido
Born in 1950. When he was in his 30s, he began learning Gyakute-do Jujutsu, which was derived from Hakkoryu Jujutsu in the 1970s. Just before reaching the age of 40, he moved from Japan to The Netherlands and continued to master and develop Gyakute-do. In October of 2013, after adding the system of Aikijutsu that he developed himself, he transformed Gyakute-do into Aiki-Jujutsu Gyakute-do, and became 2nd Soushi of Gyakute-do. After retirement, he returned to Japan and began promoting Aiki-Jujutsu Gyakute-do as his main pursuit.

[Translator's comment]
Up until now, many Jujutsu or Aikijutsu books have been published both inside and outside of Japan. But so far as I know, this book is quite unique. This book is written based on a totally different concept from other books. In this book, Okuyama 2nd Soke aims to let readers understand the concepts and philosophy of his Hakkoryu Jujutsu during the course of describing each technique. He attempts to explain the essence of each technique so deeply that all readers can understand, not only the physical technique itself, but also the concepts, and philosophy of Hakkoryu Jujutsu. Because of his strong intention to reveal the most important

points of each technique, all readers can understand Hakkoryu, even if they lack deep knowledge or experience in the art. But that is not all. The reader can begin to grasp the meaning of Hakkoryu's concepts of "no challenge, no resist and no injury". Okuyama 2nd Soke attempts to explain these concepts through his explanation of the techniques. That is the most remarkable point which distinguishes this book from all other similar books. One who reads this book can not only perform the described techniques, but they can grasp some of the deep concepts of Hakkoryu Jujutsu embedded in each of its techniques. Of course, it is impossible that anyone could master the techniques just by reading this book, but they will surely get the feeling that they have started to understand the art of Jujutsu in a much deeper sense than they did previously. I myself am such a person. I feel quite different after reading this book—not only in regard to Jujutsu techniques but also about the way in which I live my life. This is likely the result of the "mental effect" that is developed through Hakkoryu training which Okuyama Soke often mentions in this book.

●Translation collaborator
Andrew Bryant

Born in 1972. His first introduction to the martial arts began in 1983 with the study of Shorin-ryu Karatedo while growing up in Renton, Washington. He moved to Indianapolis, Indiana, in 1989 and started studying the art of Aikido. Since that time, he has studied Hakkoryu Jujutsu, Aiki-Jujutsu Gyakute-do, Iaijutsu, Jojutsu and other arts. He is the founder and chief instructor of the Indianapolis Martial Arts Center and Hakkoryu Shinwa Dojo. He continues to study and research the traditional Japanese Budo of Hakkoryu, Gyakute-do, Muso Jikiden Eishin-ryu, Shinto Muso-ryu, and associated arts.

The No.1 Japanese DVD site for Budo and Bujutsu!

Original Japanese DVD site for Budo and Bujutsu
BUDOJAPAN.COM
produced by BAB JAPAN

We offer a choice of original Japanese DVD by the greatest Japanese masters!!

Aikido, Karate, Judo, Jujutsu, Kendo, Kenjutsu, traditional Budo and Bujutsu, Ninjutsu ...

武道・武術・身体の海外向けDVD販売サイト
Japanese-origin Budo and Bujutsu DVD site
BUDOJAPAN.COM
produced by BAB JAPAN

A variety of Budo and Bujutsu DVDs performed by the Japanese greatest masters!! Go to our site for related articles.

pick up

Togakureryu The inner secrets of Ninjutsu Vol.1
34 min.
Subtitle:English

Togakureryu The inner secrets of Ninjutsu Vol.2
40 min.
Subtitle:English

Internal training for BUJUTSU VOL.1 Tetsuzan Kuroda
82min.
Language: Japanese

Internal training for BUJUTSU VOL.2 Tetsuzan Kuroda
88min.
Language: Japanese

Morihiro Saito THE AIKIDO
60min.
Subtitle:English

GOZO SHIODA'S SECRET PRINCIPLES
60min.
Subtitle:Japanese

Real Usage of PINAN KATA Okinawa Shorinryu Karate
69min.
Subtitle:English

Tenshinseiden Katorishintoryu
60 min.
Language: Japanese

pick up

KASHIMA NO HIDACHI Vol.1 SHODEN Basics
93min.
Subtitle:English

KASHIMA NO HIDACHI Vol.2 CHUDEN Intermediate
100min.
Subtitle:English

KASHIMA NO HIDACHI Vol.3 OKUDEN
103min.
Subtitle:English

Minoru Mochizuki Yoseikan General Budo Vol.1
45min.
Language: Japanese

HIRONORI OTSUKA'S WADORYU KARATE VOL.1
60 min.
Subtitle:Japanese

HIRONORI OTSUKA'S WADORYU KARATE VOL.2
60 min.
Subtitle:Japanese

CHAPTER OF OKINAWA GOJURYU VOl.1
50 min.
Language: Japanese

CHAPTER OF OKINAWA GOJURYU VOl.2
50 min.
Language: Japanese

DAITORYU AIKIJUJUTSU SECRET SYLLABUS VOL.1
45 min.
Subtitle:English

DAITORYU AIKIJUJUTSU SECRET SYLLABUS VOL.2
45 min.
Subtitle:English

DAITORYU AIKIJUJUTSU SECRET SYLLABUS VOL.3
45 min.
Subtitle:English

ONOHA ITTORYU GOKUI
40min.
Language: Japanese/ English/

MUSOJIKIDEN EISHINRYU IAI
60min.
Subtitle:Japanese/ English/

HOKUSHIN ITTORYU KENJUTSU HOKUSHIN ITTORYU KENJUTSU
40min.
Language: English

TAIZABURO NAKAMURA BATTOJUTSU PART 1
40min.
Subtitle:Japanese

TAIZABURO NAKAMURA BATTOJUTSU PART2
40min.
Subtitle:Japanese